A Switch in Time

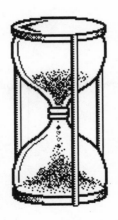

by Pamela and Matthew Granovetter

Cover by Lilo Poplilov

"A Switch in Time" was printed
in the United States of America.
Additional copies of this books may be obtained
by writing or phoning:
Granovetter Books
3194 Oak Road
Cleveland OH 44118
phone 216 371-5849
fax 216 371-2941 for credit-card orders

ISBN number 0-940257-17-3

A Switch in Time

Introduction

The following deal was reported by Eric Kokish in *Bridge Today* magazine, Nov/Dec 1993 issue.

Santiago, Chile, Bermuda Bowl 1993, Semifinals
Norway vs. Brazil

VuGraph

Last Board — Open Room
North-South Norway, East-West Brazil
Running Score: Brazil +9

East dealer
East-West vulnerable

```
                    North (Aa)
                    ♠ Q J 4 2
                    ♡ 7
                    ◊ A J 7 6 3
                    ♣ 8 4 3

West (Barbosa)                      East (Comacho)
♠ K 10 8 5                          ♠ 9 7 6
♡ A K 5 4 3        ┌──────┐         ♡ Q 8 6 2
◊ Q 4             │ 5♣X  │         ◊ K 10 9 5 2
♣ A J            └──────┘         ♣ K
                    South (Groetheim)
                    ♠ A 3
                    ♡ J 10 9
                    ◊ 8
                    ♣ Q 10 9 7 6 5 2
```

Closed Room Result: 5♣X by the Brazilian South,
down 1, +100 for Norway

"Five clubs doubled goes down only one in the closed room. The Brazilian supporters are screaming with relief and delight. How can they possibly lose now?

... The Open-Room contract flashes up. It is five clubs doubled, too. The South Americans are cheering.

"Barbosa leads the ♡A and East plays the deuce (standard attitude signals). ... Barbosa then switches to the ace of trumps, crashing the king. ...There is a hush over the room now. Barbosa has not yet continued trumps. He is wondering what Camacho's discouraging heart card was all about. Did it not say: 'Make your normal switch'?

"The normal switch appears to be a spade, looking at the dummy. Or did it say: 'Play whatever you like'?

"From Barbosa's point of view, passive defense would allow the contract to make if declarer held the ◇K and not the ♠A, and if his partner could not stand a spade switch, why didn't he play an encouraging heart at trick one?"

[At trick three, West switches to . . . the ♠8.]

"The ♠Q wins, a spade is led to the ace, a heart is ruffed, a spade is ruffed, a heart is ruffed, and the ♣Q fells the jack. South claims, for a spectacular +550 and 12 unbelievable imps to Norway — winning on the final deal, 208-205."

Why We Wrote This Book

This deal was an unhappy one for the defense (to say the least). When we first read about it, our main reaction was that we were glad it didn't happen to us! We had great sympathy for West, who, whether he misdefended or not at trick three, surely has had sleeping problems for many a night afterward.

What was the solution to the hand? In our methods, we asked ourselves, how would we have defended? Certainly East's card at trick one was an attitude signal, but which suit was it asking partner to switch to? What was the "obvious shift"?

Until this deal occured, we had some loose definitions about the Obvious Shift. When we began to discuss this hand with friends, it became apparent that determining the Obvious Shift was not the only issue — we were talking another language! "Obvious Shift?" some asked. "What the heck is that?"

Apparently, the concept is a state secret. We started to research and found it mentioned in only a few books and one or two articles. Yes, there was some literature out there, but few writers had really expounded on the subject. And, as you can see from the world championships disaster, this was an area that needed expounding! So here we go.

Three Popular Signals

The three popular signals in defensive carding are: attitude, suit preference and count. The vast majority of bridge players use these signals without firm understandings. Often two defenders are on different wavelengths, one giving one signal while the other interprets it as something else. This book is designed to clear the cobwebs of confusion. We will show how defense can be like bidding, with simple clear messages going back and forth between the two players. After you and your partner read this book, your bridge game will take a quantum leap. And you will never again return to the dark ages of guesswork.

There is only one thing we ask of you: You will have to think!

Imagine being relaxed and happy to defend contracts together, just as you are happy when the opponents stay out of your auction and you can bid unimpeded according to your system. After a little practice, imagine being able to take all your tricks on defense. Imagine that defense can be fun as well!

You will see that almost all the example hands in this book are from real-life recorded championships. We want to impress upon you the disastrous state of defensive carding and also to avoid any impression that we are making up hands to fit our carding methods. As you will see, these carding ideas are the carding methods of a few, select champions. With this book, however, the secret is finally out.

Pamela and Matthew Granovetter — May 1994

For Pat

I. Count, Attitude and No Signals

It is crucial to be able to defend well these days. Most modern bridge players use light opening bids and extremely aggressive preempts. There is no doubt that this takes a toll on their opposition. Sometimes there is no legitimate way to recover from these weapons and your side is shut out of the bidding, while they go quietly for 50-a-trick. When you are finally able to nail them with a penalty double, you absolutely must be able to take every trick in order to get back losses or build up a cushion for the times when their disruption works. And when the Meckwells of this world bid 22-point games, you must be able to defend accurately and set their contracts; otherwise you will never win.

Is Bridge a Difficult Game?

A bridge teacher we knew used to tell his students: "There are only three things wrong with your game: bidding, play and defense." Needless to say, he wasn't the most popular teacher (though he might have been the most honest). Of the three parts of bridge, defense is considered by most people the most difficult. But does this make sense? On declarer play, you are on your own against two opponents. In the bidding you are dealing with a limited code and only 13 cards. But on defense, you have a partner to help — good old partner. Even without partner, you have the exposed dummy to help you. Then there's declarer, who is often on your side as well, if you pay attention to what he is doing.

Bridge Without Signals

If you are shaking your head, saying, these authors just don't know *my* partner, let us assure you that even without a helpful partner, most defensive problems can be solved by you alone, through logic. For almost two years, we played bridge without using any defensive signaling. Our theory at the time was that signals gave declarer extra help, while all along the hand could be defeated on our own. At that time, we were playing a great deal of rubber bridge, where very little help is available anyway. We were able to figure out a defense by placing declarer with various hands that would give us a chance to defeat him, and then choosing the most probable.

Though we got by with this at the rubber bridge table, we did not succeed as well in the long run. It is exhausting to work out every single defense by yourself. It was one thing to play an evening duplicate or a session of rubber bridge this way, but it was overwhelming when we set out to play 10 days at the Nationals.

Count Signals

Let's examine the most simple signals, and see how they help. We'll begin with count, and, for the purposes of this book, we'll stick to standard carding, high-low an even number or encouraging, low-high an odd number or discouraging. (If you play upside-down, it will not affect the ideas expressed here.)

Many players use count signals and swear by them. Giving count as your primary signal has certain merit, not the least of which is that you can never make a wrong signal! We know some professionals who train their students to give count on every play — this way the student does not have to think too deeply and the pro receives some useful information that he can . . . well . . . count on.

If you can't trust your partner to know whether he likes your lead, you may prefer to stick with count (in which case, you might as well return this book to the store).

Count is very useful in certain cash-out situations, but there are many situations where count doesn't help much. After our investigatory years into the art of defense, we decided to use count in five specific situations:

(1) With a doubleton, after partner's lead of the A-K versus suit contracts — *when we want to obtain a ruff.*

(2) At the six-level, after the lead of the king.

(3) Against notrump after the lead of an ace (from A-K-J-10-x).

(4) When helping partner to hold up an ace or king.

(5) When cashing out and the highcards are known.

(1) With a doubleton, after partner's lead of the A-K versus suit contracts — *when we want to obtain a ruff.*

This is basic. For example, partner leads an ace (from A-K) and you hold the 10-3 doubleton. If you want a ruff on the third round, you play the 10 to tell partner to continue. This rule applies to a doubleton only. As you will soon see, we do not give count with a tripleton.

(2) At the six-level, after the lead of the king.

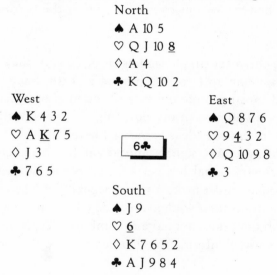

```
                    North
                    ♠ A 10 5
                    ♡ Q J 10 8
                    ♢ A 4
                    ♣ K Q 10 2
West                                East
♠ K 4 3 2                           ♠ Q 8 7 6
♡ A K 7 5           ┌─────┐         ♡ 9 4 3 2
♢ J 3               │ 6♣  │         ♢ Q 10 9 8
♣ 7 6 5             └─────┘         ♣ 3
                    South
                    ♠ J 9
                    ♡ 6
                    ♢ K 7 6 5 2
                    ♣ A J 9 8 4
```

Playing in six clubs, South receives the ♡K lead. If East gives count, by playing his second highest heart, the ♡4, he tells his partner he has an even number of hearts. West, who must guess between four and two, probably switches to a trump.*

---

*Note that East must not signal count with the very ambiguous ♡3. This is the card he would play from ♡9-4-3.

(3) Against notrump after the lead of an ace (from A-K-J-10-x).

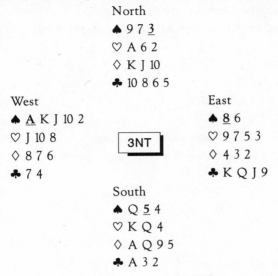

North
♠ 9 7 <u>3</u>
♡ A 6 2
◇ K J 10
♣ 10 8 6 5

West
♠ <u>A</u> K J 10 2
♡ J 10 8
◇ 8 7 6
♣ 7 4

3NT

East
♠ <u>8</u> 6
♡ 9 7 5 3
◇ 4 3 2
♣ K Q J 9

South
♠ Q <u>5</u> 4
♡ K Q 4
◇ A Q 9 5
♣ A 3 2

Against three notrump, West leads the ♠A, a special lead that asks partner to drop an honor if he has one or otherwise give count. East follows with the 8 to show an even number. West shifts and, fortunately for the defense, declarer has only eight tricks. Here the count signal is vital, but it is a special situation, which may come up at the bridge table only a few times in your life.

(4) When helping partner to hold up an ace or king.

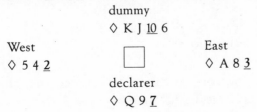

dummy
◇ K J <u>10</u> 6

West
◇ 5 4 <u>2</u>

East
◇ A 8 <u>3</u>

declarer
◇ Q 9 <u>7</u>

This is more common, though not always foolproof. Declarer attacks a long suit in dummy, where entries are sparse. For example, in the diagram, declarer leads a diamond and West signals with the ◇2 to show an odd number. East holds off until the third round. East hopes, of course, that West did not start with *five* diamonds.

(5) When cashing out and the highcards are known.

This deal was played in Biarritz, France, by the winners of the Olympiad Mixed Pairs, George Mittelman and Dianna Gordon of Canada.

South dealer
North-South vulnerable

```
                        North
                        ♠ A K 6 4
                        ♡ Q 8
                        ◇ 8 4
                        ♣ Q J 7 6 5
West                                      East
♠ J 8 7                                   ♠ 9 5 2
♡ K J 4 2        ┌──────┐                 ♡ A 10 7 5 3
◇ J 6 2          │  3◇  │                 ◇ K Q
♣ K 9 3          └──────┘                 ♣ A 8 4
                        South
                        ♠ Q 10 3
                        ♡ 9 6
                        ◇ A 10 9 7 5 3
                        ♣ 10 2
```

Mittelman		*Gordon*	
South	West	North	East
pass	pass	1 NT	double
3 ◇	(all pass)		

Mittelman went down one, and East-West scored 9 matchpoints. Down two would have meant 331 matchpoints. A trump was led. Declarer won and immediately led a heart, an attempt to make East-West think he was trying for a ruff.* East won, cashed the ◇K, and led a heart to West, who tried to cash *a third* heart. South ruffed and led four rounds of spades, discarding a club loser.

---

*Actually, if declarer ran his four spades, pitching a club, the defense would have no chance for six tricks.

What went wrong? After winning the ♡A and cashing the ◇K, East had to tell West how many hearts he held. If he returns the ♡5, West cannot know if East started with four or five hearts, because the ♡3 could be in the South hand.

East should return the ♡7, his second highest, so that West can be sure of the count. East may cash the ♣A first if he wants, but his double of one notrump clearly marked him with the two aces. Therefore the only relevant signal is count.

This deal illustrates the necessity for giving a clear count signal *when partner already knows the high-card position*. But, again, this situation is quite rare.

Attitude Signals

Most of your trick-one defensive situations will require an opinion from partner whether to continue the suit that was led. Therefore, with few exceptions, we give attitude signals when following suit to partner's lead or when discarding. This fit in well during our rubber bridge days, because almost every rubber bridge player uses simple attitude signals. By "simple" we mean an attitude signal pertaining only to the suit led. For example:

(a)	♠ J x x̲ ♡ K x x		(b)	♠ J x x̲ ♡ K x x	
♠A led	N W E S	♠ Q 8̲ 2	♠A	N W E S	♠ 10 8 2̲

(c)	♠ J x x̲ ♡ K x x		(d)	♠ J x x ♡ K x x	
♠A	N W E S	♠ Q 8 2̲ ♡ A Q J	♠A	N W E S	♠ 10 8̲ 2 ♡ x x x

West leads the ♠A (ace from ace-king) against a three-club contract. Playing simple attitude, East plays (a) the 8 from Q-8-2 and (b) the 2 from 10-8-2. He likes spades or doesn't like spades.

But suppose East wants partner to shift to hearts? On diagram (c) East really should play the ♠2. And on diagram (d) the ♠8 is the best signal, to *stop* partner from making a disastrous shift!

As you can see, simple attitude is not a good enough signal. How often have you received a discouraging signal from partner, but still had no idea how to continue? At these times you must place declarer with various advantageous holdings and choose the most probable. This can be exhausting and is by no means foolproof.

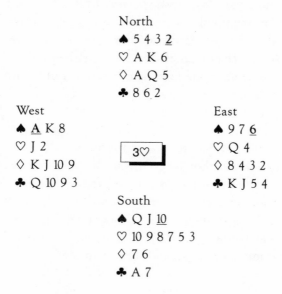

North
♠ 5 4 3 <u>2</u>
♡ A K 6
◊ A Q 5
♣ 8 6 2

West
♠ <u>A</u> K 8
♡ J 2
◊ K J 10 9
♣ Q 10 9 3

East
♠ 9 7 <u>6</u>
♡ Q 4
◊ 8 4 3 2
♣ K J 5 4

3♡

South
♠ Q J <u>10</u>
♡ 10 9 8 7 5 3
◊ 7 6
♣ A 7

On this deal from a pair event, West led the ♠A against South's three-heart contract. East signaled low and most Wests continued spades or shifted to the ◊J. Very few realized the danger of dummy's fourth spade. And only a couple of Wests found the crucial club switch, which holds the contract to 10 tricks. There is, however, an easy way to find the club switch. And if you always could find that switch on this type of hand, you would gain quite a number of matchpoints.

The solution to this defensive problem is to integrate attitude signals with the "Obvious Shift Principle." Simply put, in most situations, a discouraging signal to partner's lead shows *two* things: a) you don't like partner's suit; and b) if partner so desires, you can stand for him to make the "obvious" shift — the side suit that appears to be best for the defense to attack.

Thus, on this hand, East plays low on the spade lead, discouraging a spade continuation and inviting a club shift.

The Obvious Shift Principle is not a difficult concept, but it requires thought by both defenders. You don't have to change all your signals, which you are comfortable with and have used for many years. You merely have to *add it to your repertoire.*

Of course, the Obvious Shift Principle will not always work perfectly. No signaling system will *always* work. For example, in the last hand, if dummy's minors were reverse, diamonds would be the "obvious shift," and East would not be able to signal for a club switch. However, as you will soon see, this signaling method often leads to huge gains and rarely causes a loss.

The following hand is from Hugh Kelsey's "Advanced Play At Bridge."* The chapter is called "Camouflage" and Mr. Kelsey gives some tips on making the defense tough for the opponents.

```
                    North
                    ♠ Q 10 7 4 2
                    ♡ 6 3
                    ◇ A 5
                    ♣ K J 10 4
        ◇ 6                         ◇ 8
                    South
                    ♠ K 8 6 5 3
                    ♡ A Q 10 5
                    ◇ J
                    ♣ 7 5 2
```

South	North
1 ♠	4 ♠

"West leads the ◇6 against your four-spade contract and East drops the ◇8 under dummy's ace. How should you continue?"

Kelsey says that if the ♡K and ♣Q are poorly placed, you are in trouble. His solution is to make West guess.

"There is a chance that West will have the bare ♠A, in which case, if you take away his easy exit in diamonds before putting him in, he may have an awkward guess to make. At trick two you should ruff dummy's second diamond and then lead the ♠K."

*Faber and Faber, 1968, page 74

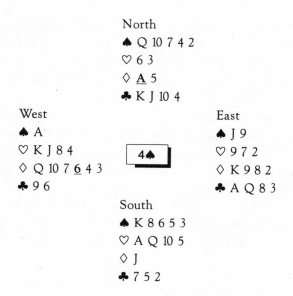

North
♠ Q 10 7 4 2
♡ 6 3
◇ A 5
♣ K J 10 4

West
♠ A
♡ K J 8 4
◇ Q 10 7 6 4 3
♣ 9 6

4♠

East
♠ J 9
♡ 9 7 2
◇ K 9 8 2
♣ A Q 8 3

South
♠ K 8 6 5 3
♡ A Q 10 5
◇ J
♣ 7 5 2

"The hand cropped up in a Gold Cup match in 1964 and Kenneth Konstam earned a game swing for his team by giving an opponent the chance to go wrong. The West player had an unenviable decision to make when in with the ♠A. From his point of view, either a heart or a club return could be right, depending on his partner's holding in the suits. Eventually he led a heart and the hand was over.

"Deceptive technique often involves no more than playing on the ignorance and the fears of your opponents. If you force them to guess, they will guess wrong half of the time."

An analysis of this deal demonstrates much of what *this* book is about. A light opening bid has made life difficult for East-West. It is imperative that they defeat the four-spade contract.

We'll look at the hand from the vantage point of the popular signaling methods, count and simple attitude; then we'll look at how you might defend if you were playing no signals.

1. Count. East gives count with the ◇9. (He should never give count with the 8 because he could have been dealt K-9-8 third. To repeat: When giving count, make it clear by playing the second highest from four.)

At trick two, when declarer leads a diamond from dummy, East may follow with the deuce (knowing that declarer does not hold the $\Diamond$ Q-J or else he would have ducked at trick one). East has now completed his count signal. He is probably happy for West to win the second trick, if possible. On the other hand, he might go up with the $\Diamond$ K at trick two in order to play a heart through. He'll feel confident that partner will play him for the missing diamond deuce and know he holds an even number of diamonds from his first play of the 9.

Meanwhile, South ruffs the second diamond and plays his ♠K. West wins his ace, but has received no help at all and must solve this problem in the same way that the signal-less player will (see below).

2. Simple Attitude. East gives simple attitude by playing the $\Diamond$ 9. At trick two he follows with the king or deuce and, again, South ruffs and plays the ♠K. West knows that East likes diamonds, but that won't help much here. West is in the same boat as the West who received count; both will have to revert to working out this hand alone, as will the signal-less West.

3. No Signals. Welcome to the world of no signals. The signal-less West didn't pay much attention to his partner's first card (because it was random), but did notice that declarer ruffed the second diamond. This West is also in with his trump ace at trick three and also has had no help from his partner thus far, but at least he never expected any. He sees that his side will need three tricks between clubs and hearts and he begins to ponder on how to take them.

It will be necessary to play South for a light opening bid, otherwise breaking the contract will be hopeless. There are two possible high-card holdings to place with East in order to defeat this contract:

(a) The $\heartsuit$A and ♣Q. West shifts to a heart, East returns a heart, West gets out with a third heart, and declarer misguesses the ♣Q.

(b) The ♣A-Q. West shifts to a club. East will win his club honors and declarer will eventually take a losing finesse in hearts.

West has probably been "in the tank" for several minutes

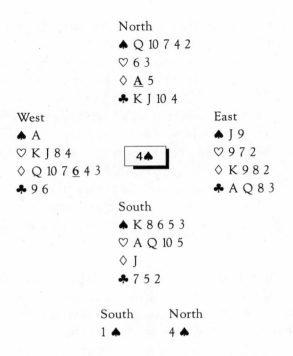

North
♠ Q 10 7 4 2
♡ 6 3
◇ **A** 5
♣ K J 10 4

West
♠ A
♡ K J 8 4
◇ Q 10 7 **6** 4 3
♣ 9 6

4♠

East
♠ J 9
♡ 9 7 2
◇ K 9 8 2
♣ A Q 8 3

South
♠ K 8 6 5 3
♡ A Q 10 5
◇ J
♣ 7 5 2

South	North
1 ♠	4 ♠

already. On the one hand, playing partner for the ♣A-Q is better, because that is a sure down one. On the other hand, if South holds the ♣A, and you destroy partner's ♣Q, he will not be a happy partner, and you will feel pretty sick yourself for the rest of the session. Though West should probably opt for the club shift, most players will shift to hearts. They would rather die a thousand deaths than lead into dummy's K-J-10-4 suit, and instead will comfort themselves by saying it's anti-percentage for partner to hold two honors in clubs, as Kenneth Konstam's opponent did.

Imagine the extra torture this hand would offer at matchpoints! There one has to take into consideration the possibility of overtricks as well.

Even if you defended this hand correctly at the table, you probably spent at least five minutes working at it. You pick up the next hand feeling pretty good about things, but also somewhat tired.

II. The Obvious Shift Principle to the Rescue

Now let's look at the last hand using the Obvious Shift Principle. East plays the ◊9 at trick one. West knows his partner likes diamonds, or, if he doesn't, he can't stand the Obvious Shift (hearts, dummy's weaker side suit).

The hand is now over!

The defense can no longer go wrong.

West knows that South holds the ♡A. When declarer ruffs a diamond and leads the ♠K, West wins his ace and sees that his only chance to defeat the contract is if East holds the ♣A-Q.

Suit Preference After Trick One

You will see in the next chapter how Suit-Preference signals take over the defense's signaling after trick one. As a preview, notice what happens on this deal at trick two. When declarer plays the second diamond from dummy, East should follow with the deuce, *suit-preference*. (East knows declarer did not begin with the ◊Q-J, else he would have ducked the opening lead.) West sees declarer ruff the diamond and knows his partner could have followed to the second diamond play with the king, 8 or 2. His choice of the deuce shows *a definite preference* for clubs.

Time out for a review.

The Obvious Shift Principle is based on the signal you have been playing for most of your bridge life: attitude. It just adds a little spice to it.

On the opening lead, when third hand has a choice of plays, he can tell his partner whether he likes the suit led. A low card shows a negative "attitude" and a high card shows a positive "attitude." However, if you are looking *only at the suit led*, and send a signal based on your holding *solely* in that suit, you are not conveying enough information. You must think harder. You must ask your-self: "Does continuing this suit help us?" and "Do I want partner to shift to another suit?" The answer to the second question might be "yes," even if you have a great deal of strength in the suit partner led!

Thus, the attitude signal at trick one is not about partner's suit in isolation; it is an indication of whether you would like a continuation or whether you would like a switch to the "obvious," or "weaker," side suit.

What does it mean that you would like a switch or *can stand* the Obvious Shift?

It means that the opening leader can shift to the obvious-shift suit from *any* holding and not lose a trick (you hope).

Here are four main examples. Assume you are behind the dummy and that you want to signal for the Obvious Shift.

obvious-shift suit	the minimum you must hold to encourage
J x x or weaker	the ace or king (or queen vs. notrump)
Q x x	the ace or king
K x x	the ace or queen
A x x	the king or queen

Please note: Sometimes the obvious-shift suit is not clear. We will get to this in chapter five. For now, we are defining the obvious-shift suit as the suit that partner might want to switch to. When it is not clear, we treat the lower ranking suit as the obvious-shift suit. (This rule was given to us by Karen McCallum.)

When You Want Partner to Switch to the Non-Obvious Suit

Suppose you want your partner to shift, but to the non-obvious suit (for example, dummy's strong or long suit). Play an unusual honor card. This is not always possible but sometimes it is. For example, you have raised partner's opening one-heart bid with ♡J-8-4 and this is the layout:

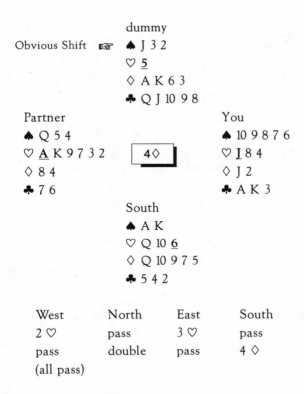

dummy
Obvious Shift ☞ ♠ J 3 2
♡ <u>5</u>
◇ A K 6 3
♣ Q J 10 9 8

Partner   You
♠ Q 5 4   ♠ 10 9 8 7 6
♡ <u>A</u> K 9 7 3 2   │ 4◇ │   ♡ J 8 4
◇ 8 4   ◇ J 2
♣ 7 6   ♣ A K 3

South
♠ A K
♡ Q 10 <u>6</u>
◇ Q 10 9 7 5
♣ 5 4 2

West	North	East	South
2 ♡	pass	3 ♡	pass
pass	double	pass	4 ◇
(all pass)			

Partner starts with a high heart. You can play the ♡8 to encourage partner to continue hearts, the ♡4 to show tolerance for the Obvious Shift (dummy's weaker side suit, spades), or the ♡J, an unusual card, asking partner to make an unusual shift (clubs). In this case, you would signal with the jack and partner would shift to clubs. His spot card tells you he holds a doubleton, so you continue the suit and give him a ruff on the third round to defeat the contract.*

Suppose you don't particularly like partner's suit, but have weak holdings in the other two suits. Here you are forced to encourage, because the alternative, a shift, is much worse. For example, on the above hand, partner leads a high heart and you hold the ♣K but not the ace. Play the ♡8 at trick one. This merely says: Don't switch to the obvious-shift suit (spades).

Let's change the last hand more dramatically:

_____

*Your ♡J would show the ♡10 only after the ♡K lead (from K-Q) when dummy does *not* have a singleton.

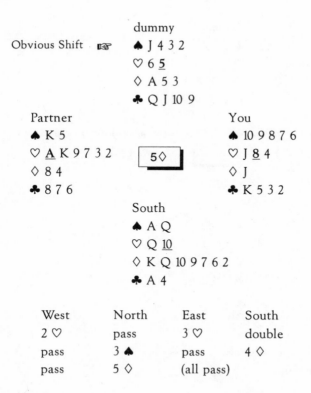

dummy

Obvious Shift ☞ ♠ J 4 3 2
♡ 6 <u>5</u>
◇ A 5 3
♣ Q J 10 9

Partner
♠ K 5
♡ <u>A</u> K 9 7 3 2
◇ 8 4
♣ 8 7 6

5◇

You
♠ 10 9 8 7 6
♡ J <u>8</u> 4
◇ J
♣ K 5 3 2

South
♠ A Q
♡ Q <u>10</u>
◇ K Q 10 9 7 6 2
♣ A 4

West	North	East	South
2 ♡	pass	3 ♡	double
pass	3 ♠	pass	4 ◇
pass	5 ◇	(all pass)	

This time the contract is five diamonds, and again partner leads a high heart. If you could stand a spade shift (the obvious-shift suit), you would play low (the ♡4). This would be your play if you held the ♠A instead of the ♣K.

On this hand, you play the ♡8, encouraging a heart continuation. Partner continues with a high heart on which you play the ♡J. Now partner *is sure* you didn't start with a doubleton, *and he also is sure* that you couldn't stand a spade switch, or else why would you have encouraged? He switches safely to a trump and declarer must lose a spade trick for down one.

Applying the Obvious Shift Principle
Situation A: Partner leads against a suit
contract and will probably hold the trick.
Third hand determines what the Obvious
Shift is and plays accordingly:

> high spot card = encouraging — I cannot stand the
> obvious shift
> low spot card = discouraging — please make the
> obvious shift*
> unusual honor card = please make an unusual shift

Situation "A" includes cases where dummy has a singleton or void in the suit led. After all, there are often situations where the best defense is to force dummy to ruff at trick two, or where any shift would be dangerous (as in the previous five-diamond hand). Although the universal signaling method when dummy has a singleton is to give suit preference, we find it easier to be consistent and stick to our normal signaling methods. Thus, most people play that if dummy has a singleton, a low card by third-hand is suit preference for the lower-ranking suit and a high card is suit preference for the higher-ranking suit.** This does not take into account the times partner wants a continuation. In general we find it is easier to use the same methods in every situation, rather than incorporate a set of exceptions. More important, these days everyone is playing transfers, and, as we know from our early lessons in defense, the best defense is often a forcing defense. When dummy has the long trumps, the forcing defense is often overlooked:

---

*What do you do when you can't stand the Obvious Shift but you can't stand a continuation either? You must choose the signal you think will be less costly. As we said before, no signaling system will *always*
Chapter VII — Troubleshooting, for exceptions to the rules.
**Let's clarify this issue. It may be easier to play high for a high suit and low for a low suit, but it is very much inferior. When the higher ranking suit is the Obvious Shift, we play low to ask for it. Likewise, when the lower ranking suit is the Obvious Shift, we play low to ask for it. A low card is an easier signal to use. If you must play an honor to get the higher-ranking suit, you will often be in difficulty, either because you weren't dealt an honor or because you can't afford to throw the honor. Therefore, we reserve the honor as a signal for the non-obvious shift, which is a rare occurrence.

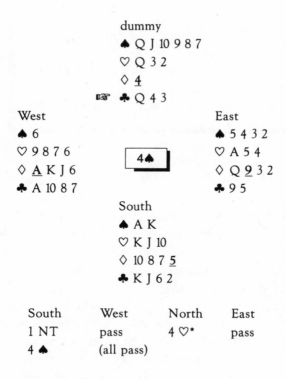

dummy
♠ Q J 10 9 8 7
♡ Q 3 2
◇ <u>4</u>
☞ ♣ Q 4 3

West
♠ 6
♡ 9 8 7 6
◇ <u>A</u> K J 6
♣ A 10 8 7

4♠

East
♠ 5 4 3 2
♡ A 5 4
◇ Q <u>9</u> 3 2
♣ 9 5

South
♠ A K
♡ K J 10
◇ 10 8 7 <u>5</u>
♣ K J 6 2

South	West	North	East
1 NT	pass	4 ♡*	pass
4 ♠	(all pass)		

*Texas transfer

West leads a top diamond and East should play the ◇9. West continues diamonds and declarer simply has no chance. Whoever wins the next trick for the defense plays a third round of diamonds. Dummy is tapped out.

Applying the Obvious Shift Principle
Situation B: Partner leads against a suit contract and declarer or dummy will win the trick.

Signal exactly as before.
High encourages and says keep away from the Obvious Shift. Low discourages and invites the Obvious Shift.
An unusual card asks for the non-obvious shift.

Suppose partner leads the ♡J and dummy's hearts are ♡A-K-Q. If you cannot stand the Obvious Shift, follow with a high spot card.

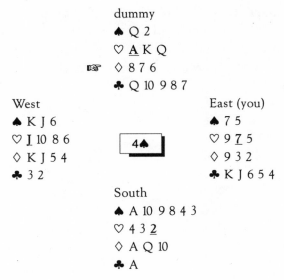

dummy
♠ Q 2
♡ <u>A</u> K Q
☞ ◊ 8 7 6
♣ Q 10 9 8 7

West
♠ K J 6
♡ <u>J</u> 10 8 6
◊ K J 5 4
♣ 3 2

4♠

East (you)
♠ 7 5
♡ 9 <u>7</u> 5
◊ 9 3 2
♣ K J 6 5 4

South
♠ A 10 9 8 4 3
♡ 4 3 <u>2</u>
◊ A Q 10
♣ A

Against four spades, West leads the ♡J. East should signal encouraging (the 7, or even the 9). He does not want a shift. Suppose that declarer wins and tries the ♠Q. This loses to West's king. West now knows not to shift and continues safely with a heart. Declarer is helpless and must rely on diamond finesses, which lose.

Partner can see that you don't like hearts, but your high spot card warns him not to shift from his honor holdings when he regains the lead. To repeat, if dummy offers no future in the suit led, an encouraging spot card still suggests a continuation is best.

Thinking is Part of the Game

Perhaps the most interesting aspect of the Obvious Shift signal is that your play at trick one is no longer automatic. You have to think. This, of course, can be dangerous. As a bridge pro once told us, "I instruct all my students to give count. That way they don't have to think and I can usually rely on the information I receive."

A few years ago, we wrote an editorial in *Bridge Today* magazine (March/April '91 issue) about this very subject. It was then when we first advocated the attitude signal as the primary defensive carding agreement and first discussed the Obvious Shift Principle with all its thought-provoking implications. In the editorial we presented the following deal, which was played at the ACBL 1990 Fall Nationals in San Francisco. It demonstrates a spectacular subtlety of the attitude signal and obvious-shift principle. East was Mike Lawrence, West was Matthew Granovetter.

South dealer
Both sides vulnerable

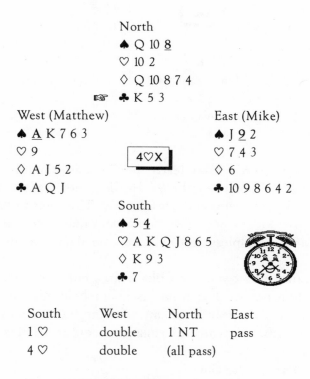

North
♠ Q 10 8
♡ 10 2
◊ Q 10 8 7 4
☞ ♣ K 5 3

West (Matthew)
♠ A K 7 6 3
♡ 9
◊ A J 5 2
♣ A Q J

4♡X

East (Mike)
♠ J 9 2
♡ 7 4 3
◊ 6
♣ 10 9 8 6 4 2

South
♠ 5 4
♡ A K Q J 8 6 5
◊ K 9 3
♣ 7

South	West	North	East
1 ♡	double	1 NT	pass
4 ♡	double	(all pass)	

Opening lead: ♠A (ace from ace-king)

First consider the deal from West's angle. As soon as dummy appeared, West was anxious to shift to clubs — he had no idea East held six of them — in order to set up a possible second club trick before the ♠Q was established for a discard. Had East signaled with the ♠2 — 99% of all bridge players *would* follow with the deuce — West would have shifted to ace and another club, whereupon declarer would win in dummy (discarding a spade), draw trumps and make his doubled contract.

Now let's look at the deal from Mike's angle. When dummy appeared, it was his viewpoint that if West held the ◊A or ♡A, a diamond shift would produce diamond ruffs for the defense. However, if he discouraged in spades, West was unlikely to shift to diamonds, because the Obvious Shift appeared to be clubs. Therefore Mike encouraged in spades by playing the ♠9. He wasn't thrilled with a spade continuation, but he hated the look of a club switch — how right he was!

Back to West's viewpoint. When West saw the ♠9, it appeared to be a doubleton, so he continued spades. However, when East followed to the second trick with the ♠J, West stopped in his tracks. Why, West thought, had Mike encouraged at trick one when he held three spades? Obviously, because he didn't want to discourage — *he didn't want a club shift*. Thus, West cashed the ◊A and led a diamond. Mike ruffed, returned a club to West's ace and received a second diamond ruff. That amounted to six tricks for the defense, 800 points.

Now we know that there are expert players who swear by "count at trick one." And they would argue that by playing the ♠2 on the first trick, West could cash a second spade to receive a suit-preference signal at trick two. But would he? It is very tempting to shift to clubs before cashing the second spade. (If declarer held three clubs instead of three diamonds, West would lose a trick by cashing the ♠K before shifting to clubs.) Also, if East held four spades, how would his count signal at trick one distinguish between four cards and a doubleton?

Is bridge a game where you derive pleasure from "following suit" without thinking? Or would you prefer a method of card play in which you can express your opinion, too? Our view is that giving count is easier than giving attitude, but so is pulling the cards from the dummy easier than declaring. Which do you prefer?

Problems

Here are 10 situations in which you are sitting over the dummy and must make a vital signal at trick one. In all 10 cases, they play in four spades after South opened the bidding one spade and no other suit was mentioned. Partner leads the ♡A (from ace-king). Your mission is to identify the Obvious Shift, then decide which card to play at trick one. As you will see, without some clear guidelines, the Obvious Shift will not always be apparent. In the answers, you will learn some of our rules for identifying the Obvious Shift. (More detailed rules will appear in Chapter 5.)

Problem 1.

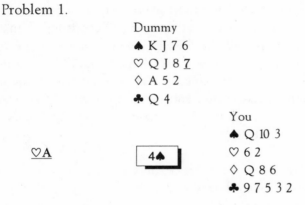

Dummy
♠ K J 7 6
♡ Q J 8 <u>7</u>
◊ A 5 2
♣ Q 4

♡A

4♠

You
♠ Q 10 3
♡ 6 2
◊ Q 8 6
♣ 9 7 5 3 2

1. The Obvious Shift is diamonds. Against a suit contract, we play that a three-card suit *headed by at most one honor* is the Obvious Shift, even if there is a shorter or weaker side suit.

2. Play the ♡2. The rule for giving count with a doubleton after partner's lead of an ace-king is that you give count *if you want a ruff*. Here you have a natural trump trick and, therefore, no reason to ask partner to continue.

This hand illustrates the difference between signaling like a robot or like a thinking player. You don't mind a diamond switch, and it may be vital when partner holds the ◊K.

Problem 2.

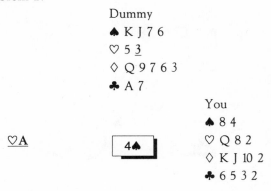

Dummy
♠ K J 7 6
♡ 5 <u>3</u>
◇ Q 9 7 6 3
♣ A 7

You
♠ 8 4
♡ Q 8 2
◇ K J 10 2
♣ 6 5 3 2

♡**A**   4♠

1. The Obvious Shift is clubs, the shorter side suit, when no weak three-card suit is in dummy.

2. Play the ♡8. You like hearts and hate clubs, so encourage in hearts. The ♡Q would show the ♡J and invite partner to underlead. This signal is universal, and we still use it. Thus, you cannot ask for an unusual shift here. (If dummy held a *singleton* heart, you could signal the queen for a diamond shift.)

Problem 3.

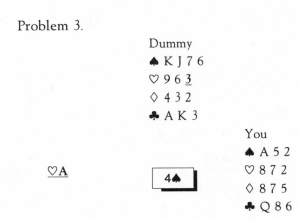

Dummy
♠ K J 7 6
♡ 9 6 <u>3</u>
◇ 4 3 2
♣ A K 3

You
♠ A 5 2
♡ 8 7 2
◇ 8 7 5
♣ Q 8 6

♡**A**   4♠

1. The Obvious Shift is diamonds, the weaker of equal-length suits.

2. Play the ♡7 because you can't stand a diamond shift. You will continue with the ♡8 so partner knows you didn't start with a doubleton. Partner may blow a heart trick, but only if he led from ♡A-K-J-x. The diamond switch would almost certainly cost.

Problem 4.

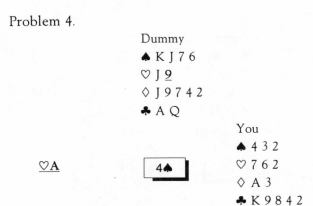

Dummy
♠ K J 7 6
♡ J 9
◇ J 9 7 4 2
♣ A Q

You
♠ 4 3 2
♡ 7 6 2
◇ A 3
♣ K 9 8 4 2

♡A   4♠

1. The Obvious Shift is clubs. Although dummy's club strength is much greater than the diamond strength, the shorter suit is the Obvious Shift.

2. Play the ♡2. You certainly want to take your club trick before declarer's (possible) ♡Q is set up for a club pitch.

Problem 5.

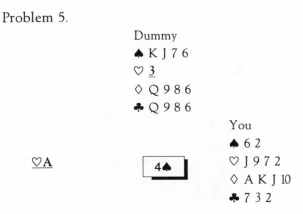

Dummy
♠ K J 7 6
♡ 3
◇ Q 9 8 6
♣ Q 9 8 6

You
♠ 6 2
♡ J 9 7 2
◇ A K J 10
♣ 7 3 2

♡A   4♠

1. The Obvious Shift is clubs. When two suits are relatively equal, the lower ranking is deemed the Obvious Shift.

2. Play the ♡J. You are desperate for a diamond switch, so you play an unusual heart card asking for an unusual shift. In fact, declarer's hand was: ♠ A Q 10 9 8 ♡ Q 4 ◇ 4 3 2 ♣ A K J, so if you don't get those diamonds now, they'll make four spades.

Problem 6.

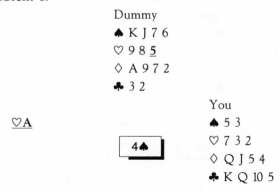

Dummy

♠ K J 7 6
♡ 9 8 <u>5</u>
◇ A 9 7 2
♣ 3 2

♡A

4♠

You

♠ 5 3
♡ 7 3 2
◇ Q J 5 4
♣ K Q 10 5

1. The Obvious Shift is clubs.

2. Play the ♡2. You will not necessarily get a club switch. Partner, knowing you have something in clubs, may switch to a trump. Remember: Partner uses the information you provide him with; he is not forced to switch. If you show strength in dummy's short suit, it is often right for partner to switch to trumps.

Problem 7.

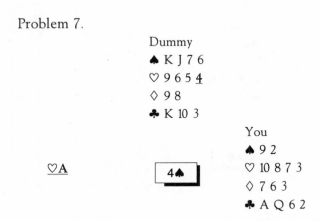

Dummy

♠ K J 7 6
♡ 9 6 5 <u>4</u>
◇ 9 8
♣ K 10 3

You

♠ 9 2
♡ 10 8 7 3
◇ 7 6 3
♣ A Q 6 2

♡A

4♠

1. The Obvious Shift is diamonds. Clubs would be the Obvious Shift if dummy held only one club honor.

2. Play the ♡8, encouraging. Partner will soon discover your heart length and will realize that you don't love hearts, but merely can't stand the Obvious Shift. When you follow suit in trumps, you will play the 2-9 to indicate suit preference for clubs.

Problem 8.

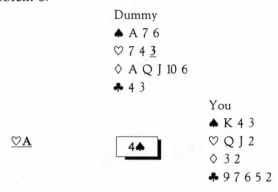

Dummy
♠ A 7 6
♡ 7 4 <u>3</u>
◇ A Q J 10 6
♣ 4 3

You
♠ K 4 3
♡ Q J 2
◇ 3 2
♣ 9 7 6 5 2

♡A   4♠

1. The Obvious Shift is, obviously, clubs.

2. Play the ♡Q, promising the ♡J. You would like to win the second trick in order to play a club through the declarer. Remember, when partner leads the ace from ace-king, your queen shows the jack; it is not a signal.

Problem 9.

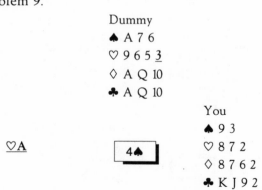

Dummy
♠ A 7 6
♡ 9 6 5 <u>3</u>
◇ A Q 10
♣ A Q 10

You
♠ 9 3
♡ 8 7 2
◇ 8 7 6 2
♣ K J 9 2

♡A   4♠

1. The Obvious Shift is clubs, the lower ranking of two equal suits.

2. Play the ♡2. This is easy.

Problem 10.

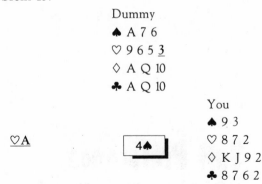

Dummy
♠ A 7 6
♡ 9 6 5 <u>3</u>
◇ A Q 10
♣ A Q 10

You
♠ 9 3
♡ 8 7 2
◇ K J 9 2
♣ 8 7 6 2

♡A

4♠

1. The Obvious Shift is clubs, again.

2. The normal play is the ♡7, followed by the ♡8. In this case, however, the ♡7 would be very costly if partner had exactly ♡A-K-J alone and continued. No matter what signaling system you use, common sense comes first. It is better to signal with the ♡2, because the club shift will give nothing away. You will play the ♣2 if partner shifts to clubs and the ♠9-3 when following suit in trumps, to show diamond strength. If partner continues hearts, you will follow with the ♡8, suit preference for diamonds.

~

In these 10 problems we learned some rules for identifying the Obvious Shift.

Without bidding to guide us, against a suit contract the Obvious Shift is (in order of priority):
• a three-card suit in dummy headed by at most one honor
• dummy's shorter side suit, but not a singleton or void
• the weaker of equal length suits
• the shorter side suit, even when it is stronger than another suit
• the lower-ranking suit when you are in doubt

Against notrump, however, the Obvious Shift is the shortest suit in dummy.

III. Suit Preference, Obvious Shift's Big Brother

I f the obvious-shift signal at trick one is "little brother" getting a chance to say something first, suit preference for the entire rest of the hand is "big brother" taking over. The signal at trick one, whether you can stand the Obvious Shift, is nice because it may be important for the opening leader to have that information before the play to trick two. It may also be the last chance third-hand gets to tell partner if he wants a switch, but this is not likely. Most of the time, the defense gets another chance or two, or three, to inform each other about vital information in the other suits. The easiest way to give this information is by signaling suit preference while following suit to the declarer's choice of plays.

Here, count givers are losing out. Though it is occasionally important to give count in the suit declarer attacks, it is usually more important to tell partner where your strength lies.

During our rubber bridge days, we noticed that we spent a lot of time following suit to *their* suits, without signaling. It seemed like a waste of opportunity. Even at duplicate, when we gave careful count, it seemed silly, because most of the time it served no purpose. One day the following deal came up:

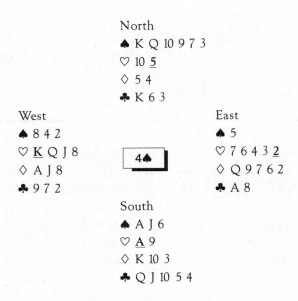

North
♠ K Q 10 9 7 3
♡ 10 <u>5</u>
◇ 5 4
♣ K 6 3

West
♠ 8 4 2
♡ <u>K</u> Q J 8
◇ A J 8
♣ 9 7 2

4♠

East
♠ 5
♡ 7 6 4 3 <u>2</u>
◇ Q 9 7 6 2
♣ A 8

South
♠ A J 6
♡ <u>A</u> 9
◇ K 10 3
♣ Q J 10 5 4

Playing in a matchpoint event, most Souths were in four spades after an opening one notrump by South and transfer by North. West led the ♡K. At our table, declarer drew trumps in three rounds and led a club to the queen, followed by a club to the king. East won the ♣A and, afraid that South held the ◇A, continued with a heart before the heart loser was discarded on the clubs.

We heard that at one table declarer cleverly attacked clubs at trick two. East won his ace and returned a heart.

Was there something we could think of to solve East's problem?

We were able to solve this problem and are now able to make maximum use of defensive signaling on every single bridge hand we defend! For the situations in which we were lazily giving count or simply following suit, we began to give suit-preference signals. For example, when declarer pulls trumps or attacks his long suit, we help partner by signaling where our strength lies.

On this hand, it is easy for East to switch to a diamond after declarer pulls trumps. Wests begs for a diamond switch simply by going up the line in trumps. If declarer wins the first trick and leads a club to the king at trick two, West again signals for a diamond by following suit with the deuce, a suit preference signal, not a count signal.

> ### Applying Suit Preference
> When following with small cards in declarer's suit, choose
> between high-low (showing strength in a high-ranking suit)
> or low-high (showing strength in a low-ranking suit).

When holding three or more cards in declarer's suit, you can
actually show many and various holdings. The difficult thing to
remember is that this is informative, not demanding; partner is not
obligated to play the suit where the positive suit preference was
shown. He is to use the information in context of the whole hand.

You will still be giving count when it appears that it is *vital* for
partner to hold up an honor. But your general reflex will be to give
suit preference. Though count sometimes helps partner to analyze
a hand, suit preference is frequently more successful and *much
easier* for partner to apply. The following deal is from Kit Woolsey's
thought-provoking booklet, "Modern Defensive Signaling in Contract Bridge," published 14 years ago (Devyn Press, page 12).

```
                          North
                          ♠ 7 5 4
                          ♡ K Q 7
                          ◇ A J 10
                          ♣ Q 7 6 5
        West                                East
        ♠ 6 3 2                             ♠ J 10 9 8
        ♡ 10 8 4 2        ┌─────┐           ♡ J 5 3
        ◇ 8 4 2           │ 3NT │           ◇ K 7
        ♣ A 10 4          └─────┘           ♣ K J 8 2
                          South
                          ♠ A K Q
                          ♡ A 9 6
                          ◇ Q 9 6 5 3
                          ♣ 9 3
```

South	West	North	East
1 NT	pass	3 NT	(all pass)

West leads a heart to East's jack and South's ace. South plays the ♢Q to East's king. East must now decide whether to shift to spades or clubs.

Woolsey says that West's count signal in diamonds helps East to shift to clubs. South appears to hold five diamonds (West shows three) and is known to hold three heart winners, for a total of seven tricks. And that accounts for only six of his minimum 15 points.

"If he has the ace of clubs, he will always have nine tricks, since he has at least the king and queen of spades. Therefore, the club shift is the only chance."

This conclusion is sound only for rubber bridge or teams. At matchpoints, East can't afford to lead back a club on the *hope* that South's points are all in spades. Also, the reasoning that led to the club shift is a bit complicated, and we all know players who are not up to such deep analysis.

Now try suit preference. There is no reason for West to give East the diamond count. East is not really interested in holding up his king. He is more interested what to do after winning the trick. The simple and clear message West should give is: "My strength is in clubs." His play of the ♢2 *on the first round of diamonds* tells East that he holds a club honor. This is happy news for East, who, without further analysis, can safely switch to the ♣2, whether the game is imps or matchpoints.

On Partner's Lead at Trick Two

Suit-preference signals are commonly used when one defender tries to give partner a ruff. We've all used these signals many times. In today's bridge world, suit preference is being applied much more frequently, especially by the top players. Suit preference in the trump suit* has become very popular and many experts use suit preference *at trick two* after the defense holds the first trick.

---

*When you play suit preference in the trump suit, you must give up the classic trump-echo signal, showing three trumps or a desire to ruff. That signal, however, is rarely useful, whereas suit preference comes up on every hand.

The following deal is from the final of the 1993 Spingold Team Championships. Both East-West partnerships solved the defense because of suit preference.

East dealer
Neither side vulnerable

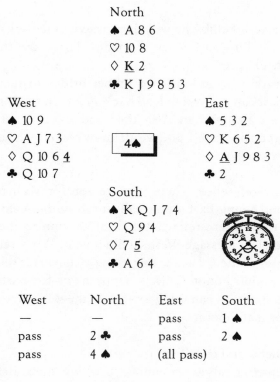

North
♠ A 8 6
♡ 10 8
♢ K 2
♣ K J 9 8 5 3

West
♠ 10 9
♡ A J 7 3
♢ Q 10 6 4
♣ Q 10 7

4♠

East
♠ 5 3 2
♡ K 6 5 2
♢ A J 9 8 3
♣ 2

South
♠ K Q J 7 4
♡ Q 9 4
♢ 7 5
♣ A 6 4

West	North	East	South
—	—	pass	1 ♠
pass	2 ♣	pass	2 ♠
pass	4 ♠	(all pass)	

Opening lead: ♢ 4

The auction was the same at both tables and both Wests led a low diamond. Both declarers went up with dummy's ♢K. Had declarer played low from dummy, East could win the ♢J and cash the ace, while West follows with the ♢Q under the ace, suit preference for hearts.

The play of the ♢K at trick one made it more difficult on the defenders, but they prevailed. Both Easts, Nick Nickell and Zia Mahmood, won the ♢A and continued with the ♢J. It was their intention to hold the lead at trick two, and then decide whether to shift to a heart or a club. It was vital to know whether West held the ♡A or ♣A, and both Wests, Dick Freeman and Mike Rosenberg, signaled the ♡A by dropping the ◊10 under the jack. The contract was then set at both tables.

Of course, it was possible that West started with ◊Q-10-4, and had no option but to drop the ◊10 under the jack. But because there was at least a 50% chance that the ◊10 *was* a signal, both East's went with the odds by returning a heart.

Let's summarize for a moment the two main principles we've discussed.

1) At trick one, we give the Obvious Shift signal.
2) After that we give suit preference.

At trick one, we tell partner if we can stand the Obvious Shift. Thereafter suit preference helps both defenders in switching to the right suit and holding on to the right suit if declarer rattles off a lot of winners.

Can suit preference ever be used at trick one? Some partnerships say yes, when dummy is short in the suit led or when the opening leader might have led a singleton. (Confusion reigns in this area, and we will cover it in Chapter VII - Troubleshooting.) We say no, there's no suit preference at trick one, with one exception. Because we give suit preference in trumps, if partner happened to lead a trump at trick one, third hand gives suit preference.

The following deal took place in the 1990 Vanderbilt. We were kibitzing Zia when he picked up this hand:
♠ Q J 10 9 4 ♡ 4 ◊ A K ♣ A Q 9 7 3. He opened one club, and the next hand bid one spade. Double by his partner. Fourth chair said two diamonds. Now what?

There simply is no good bid at this point. So Zia took the RED
D (double) card from the bidding box and two diamonds doubled
became the final contract. He led the king of trumps and this is
what we saw:

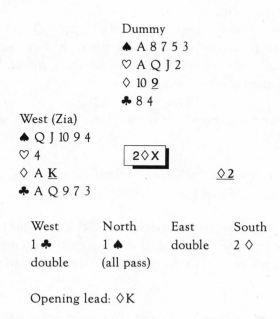

Dummy

♠ A 8 7 5 3
♡ A Q J 2
◇ 10 9
♣ 8 4

West (Zia)

♠ Q J 10 9 4
♡ 4
◇ A K
♣ A Q 9 7 3

2◇X

◇ 2

West	North	East	South
1 ♣	1 ♠	double	2 ◇
double	(all pass)		

Opening lead: ◇K

On this trick, partner played the deuce and declarer the 3. Now
what, kibitzer?

Zia shifted to . . . a spade, but declarer, who had the singleton
king, won, went to dummy in hearts and discarded a club on the
♠A. Here was the entire deal:

                          Dummy
                          ♠ A 8 7 5 3
                          ♡ A Q J 2
                          ◊ 10 <u>9</u>
                          ♣ 8 4

West (Zia)   East (Rosenberg)
♠ Q J 10 9 4   ♠ 6 2
♡ 4   ┌─────────┐   ♡ K 9 8 7 5
◊ A <u>K</u>   │ 2◊X   │   ◊ 8 6 <u>2</u>
♣ A Q 9 7 3   └─────────┘   ♣ K 10 4

                          South
                          ♠ K
                          ♡ 10 6 3
                          ◊ Q J 7 5 4 <u>3</u>
                          ♣ J 6 2

What did East mean by the ◊ 2 at trick one? We're not sure, but
we are sure what it *should* mean: suit preference for clubs.

How should West defend based on that information?

He should cash the ◊ A and switch to a low club. As you can see,
the defense would take the first five tricks and eventually score a
heart trick for down one.

A Grand Slam

One of the most exciting hands we've ever seen occurred in the
Valkenburg 1980 World Bridge Team Olympiad, in which Cana-
dian star Eric Murray was able to score a no-play grand slam
because his opponents didn't use suit preference.

South dealer
East-West vulnerable

```
                        North
                        ♠ K Q 5
                        ♡ K Q 8 7 2
                        ◇ K 2
                        ♣ A Q 4
West                                        East
♠ J 8 3 2                                   ♠ 9 7 6
♡ J 10 9 3          ┌──────┐               ♡ 4
◇ 10 7             │  7NT  │               ◇ J 9 8 6 4
♣ 6 5 2            └──────┘               ♣ J 10 7 3
                        South
                        ♠ A 10 4
                        ♡ A 6 5
                        ◇ A Q 5 3
                        ♣ K 9 8
```

Murray		*Kehela*	
South	West	North	East
1 NT	pass	2 ◇*	pass
2 NT	pass	3 ♡	pass
3 ♠	pass	4 NT	pass
5 ♠	pass	5 NT	pass
6 ◇	pass	7 NT	(all pass)

*forcing Stayman

West led the ♣6, won by declarer with the ♣K. Murray played the ♡A-K and got the bad news. His only chance to score the grand slam was for East to pitch the wrong minor-suit cards before he had information about the distribution of declarer's hand. Because declarer was known to hold only three spades on the bidding, Murray first cashed three spades and then the ♡Q.

At this point East was down to four diamonds and three clubs and he had a problem. His partner's opening lead could have been from a small doubleton or a small tripleton in clubs and East didn't know which. Perhaps West should have led the deuce of clubs, even without an honor, just to tell his partner the club count. But little did he realize the revolting developments that would ensue.

After long thought, East played Murray to hold four clubs and he threw away a second diamond, losing the grand slam.

How could West have helped?

West is known to hold four spades and four hearts. His partner is dying to know which three-card minor he holds. West can reveal his longer minor via *suit preference* — this time not for strength but for length! By following up-the-line in hearts and spades, West can show "length" in the club suit. In essence, West is saying he cannot protect diamonds.

Now suppose West had led a doubleton club and South held four clubs and three diamonds. West would play the ♡J-10 on the second and third round of hearts and give a high-low when following in spades. These signals would show a preference for diamonds, in this case diamond "length."

This was a subtle example of suit preference at the highest level, but without it, 17 imps flew South.

Speaking of subtle plays, here's a beautiful one from the Valkenburg Team Final between the USA and France, which France went on to win.

South dealer
Both sides vulnerable

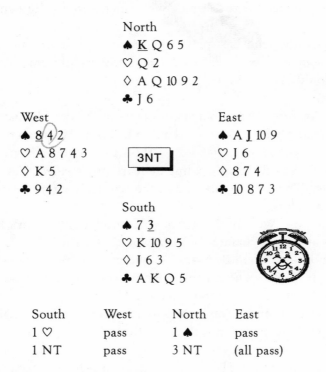

North
♠ K Q 6 5
♡ Q 2
◇ A Q 10 9 2
♣ J 6

West
♠ 8 4 2
♡ A 8 7 4 3
◇ K 5
♣ 9 4 2

3NT

East
♠ A J 10 9
♡ J 6
◇ 8 7 4
♣ 10 8 7 3

South
♠ 7 3
♡ K 10 9 5
◇ J 6 3
♣ A K Q 5

South	West	North	East
1 ♡	pass	1 ♠	pass
1 NT	pass	3 NT	(all pass)

The French West found the best lead of the ♠8. Declarer played dummy's ♠K and East the ♠J. Because communications were difficult, the declarer chose to play the ◇A and ◇9 from dummy, hoping to end up with one spade, four diamonds and four club tricks. His hope was that West would not have both missing red honors and three spades. West won the ◇K, played a spade to East's 9, won the heart return and played a third spade through, for five tricks and +100.

To defeat this contract, East had to play back the right suit after winning the ♠9. This was declarer's opening-bid heart suit, instead of the more tempting club suit. Would you have done the same?

Of course, because East's second spade play was the ♠4, suit-preference. The more common treatment is to play "remainder count" on the second round of a suit, but that would have been no help at all to East. If he thought that the ♠4 was merely a count signal, he surely would have gone wrong by returning a club.

Now you try one. You are East.

South dealer
North-South vulnerable

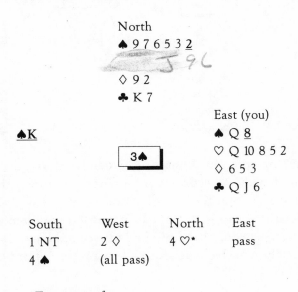

```
                    North
                    ♠ 9 7 6 5 3 2
                    ♡ J 9 6
                    ◇ 9 2
                    ♣ K 7
                                    East (you)
   ♠K                              ♠ Q 8
              ┌──────┐             ♡ Q 10 8 5 2
              │  3♠  │             ◇ 6 5 3
              └──────┘             ♣ Q J 6
```

South	West	North	East
1 NT	2 ◇	4 ♡*	pass
4 ♠	(all pass)		

*Texas transfer

Your partner leads the ♠K (South dropping the 10) and switches to the ◇K. Declarer wins the ◇A and plays a club to dummy's ♣K, a club back to the ace, and ruffs a club, partner following to all three rounds of clubs. Now declarer plays a heart to his ace and another club. Partner shows out and the second diamond is discarded from dummy, as you ruff with the ♠Q. What do you play next?

"Wait a second," you say. "I play accurate defensive signals. I need to know what my partner played on the fourth round of clubs."

Okay, fair enough. Partner discarded the ◇Q on the fourth round of clubs. What do you play?

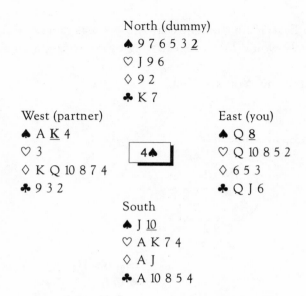

North (dummy)
♠ 9 7 6 5 3 <u>2</u>
♡ J 9 6
◇ 9 2
♣ K 7

West (partner)
♠ A <u>K</u> 4
♡ 3
◇ K Q 10 8 7 4
♣ 9 3 2

4♠

East (you)
♠ Q <u>8</u>
♡ Q 10 8 5 2
◇ 6 5 3
♣ Q J 6

South
♠ J <u>10</u>
♡ A K 7 4
◇ A J
♣ A 10 8 5 4

Partner was screaming for a heart ruff when he played the ◇ Q on declarer's high club. Return a heart for partner to ruff with the ♠ 4. This defeats the contract.

What if declarer began with three hearts and three diamonds? In that case, partner would have pitched his second heart on the fourth round of clubs, so by logic alone a heart return must be the best defense.

That one was too easy, you say. Okay. This time you are West.

East dealer
Both sides vulnerable

North
♠ Q 8
♡ 9 6 3
◊ K 10 9 5
♣ Q 10 6 <u>4</u>

West (you)
♠ A 10 7
♡ K 5 2
◊ Q 6 2
♣ K 7 5 <u>2</u>

3NT

♣8

West	North	East	South
—	—	pass	1 NT (16-19)
pass	2 ♣	pass	2 ◊*
pass	2 NT	pass	3 NT
(all pass)			

*natural, four diamonds

You lead the ♣2, low from dummy, 8 from partner, jack from declarer. Declarer plays the ♠6 to dummy's queen, and a spade back to his king and your ace. Partner has followed with the ♠5 and ♠4. Your play.

Partner is, of course, showing heart preference. You switch to the ♡2, low from dummy, jack from partner, 8 from South. Partner returns the ♡4, 10 from South, ♡K by you, low from dummy. Your play . . .

This one is tough. You have three tricks in and will need two more. Partner certainly has no more entries, which makes clearing the heart suit unattractive. If declarer's distribution is 3-3-4-3 and you continue with a third heart, declarer can play a third round of spades and three rounds of diamonds, endplaying you in clubs. You must therefore hope declarer's shape is 4-3-4-2. If so, he probably started with ♠K-J-9-6 (the 2 and 3 are still missing and it's unlikely he would have squandered the 6 from ♠K-J-6-2 or ♠K-J-6-3). Your ♠10 will drop, giving him three spade tricks, one heart, three diamonds and two clubs, for nine. Therefore, you must set up a club trick before the diamonds are established. Upon winning the ♡K, you switch to a club and finish +100.

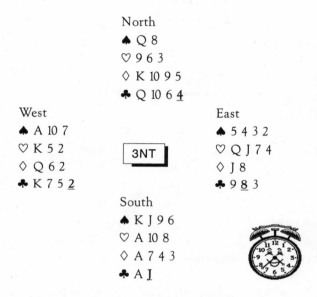

North
♠ Q 8
♡ 9 6 3
♢ K 10 9 5
♣ Q 10 6 <u>4</u>

West
♠ A 10 7
♡ K 5 2
♢ Q 6 2
♣ K 7 5 <u>2</u>

East
♠ 5 4 3 2
♡ Q J 7 4
♢ J 8
♣ 9 <u>8</u> 3

3NT

South
♠ K J 9 6
♡ A 10 8
♢ A 7 4 3
♣ A <u>J</u>

Do you think this is too difficult? Australia's Richard Cummings found this defense to defeat Poland's three notrump in the Valkenburg World Championships. True, it takes a lot of hard work, logic and some suit-preference help, but it can be done!

How to Avoid "Crashing" Honors

One of the most embarrassing plays on defense occurs when you crash your partner's honor with your honor. Yet it happens to many players, even top players. The way to avoid this costly mistake is to watch your partner's suit-preference carding carefully.

A world-class player crashed her partner's ace on this deal.

South dealer
Neither side vulnerable

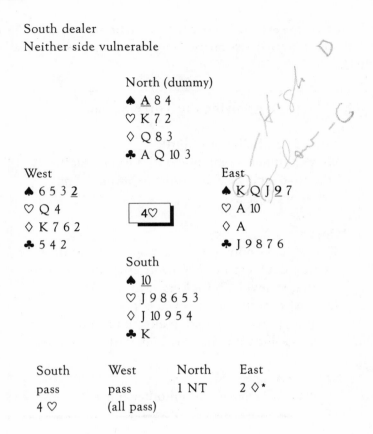

North (dummy)
♠ A 8 4
♡ K 7 2
◇ Q 8 3
♣ A Q 10 3

West
♠ 6 5 3 2
♡ Q 4
◇ K 7 6 2
♣ 5 4 2

4♡

East
♠ K Q J 9 7
♡ A 10
◇ A
♣ J 9 8 7 6

South
♠ 10
♡ J 9 8 6 5 3
◇ J 10 9 5 4
♣ K

South	West	North	East
pass	pass	1 NT	2 ◇*
4 ♡	(all pass)		

*spades and a minor

West led a spade to dummy's ace. Declarer played a club to her king, and a heart to the king and ace. East returned a high spade. Declarer ruffed and played a low diamond toward dummy's queen. Oops. West put up the king and that was -420.

We don't know what West was thinking when she rose with her ◇K, but surely something intelligent. Perhaps she thought East's minor was diamonds, and she wanted to win the ◇K to give her partner a club ruff. Or perhaps she thought declarer held the ◇A-x doubleton and was trying to sneak across her 10th trick.

In any event, East can tell her story when she returns her spade. If she is looking for a club ruff, she can return the ♠J. To show diamond preference, she returns the ♠K. After this simple signal, West knows where the ◇A is and won't make an error.

Time out for review. There are three main signals in bridge and we now have a fairly reasonable agreement on when we use each signal.

Applying the Three Signals

Attitude and Obvious Shift*
We use *attitude* combined with *Obvious Shift*:
• the first time we follow suit to *partner's lead*
• when we discard

Count
We use *count* only in five very specific instances:
• with a doubleton to get a ruff after an A-K lead
• at the six-level after a king lead
• against notrump after the ace lead
• helping partner to holdup an ace or king
• when cashing out and the highcards are known

Suit Preference
We use *suit preference* at all other times.

---

*The Obvious Shift Principle

is used with attitude signals at trick one, when third hand has the chance to make a signal.

An encouraging signal says not only do you want the opening leader to continue but, "From my point of view, I don't want you to shift to dummy's 'weakness' (the Obvious Shift)." A low card says, "I wouldn't mind if you made the Obvious Shift."

IV. Kibitzing
at the World Team Olympiad

Salsomaggiore, September, 1992 — Welcome to the Olympiad
Teams. It's an exciting affair, and Italy in September can be
quite delightful. Unfortunately, this particular September the
weather was excruciatingly hot, and even the chilled white wines
of Sicily were not enough to cool you off. Still, the kibitzers had
more fun than many of the players, because the deals are much
easier to handle when you are not the one in the hot seat.

Let's journey to some of the tables and see what happens. It's
amazing how many defenses go wrong even at this level of
competition. Many of the errors could be avoided by Obvious-
Shift and suit-preference methods. But then, this book was written
after our visit to Italy.

Ahh, there's Meckwell, the famous American pair. We'll begin
with an example of a beautiful defense by Jeff Meckstroth and Eric
Rodwell. For years they have been playing methods similar to
those described in this book. (You will later see that Hamman and
Wolff also use these methods. In fact, many champions use them
and for some it has become second nature.) This hand took place
in a qualifying match against Pakistan. Lucky you, there's a vacant
seat between South and East. Hurry, the bidding is almost over,

but you have time to see the auction before they pick up the bidding cards and put them in their boxes.

East dealer
East-West vulnerable

```
                        North
                        ♠ 10 9 8 7
                        ♡ Q J 8 3
                        ◇ A Q 10 2
                        ♣ 5
West (Meckstroth)                       East (Rodwell)
♠ Q 5 4                                 ♠ K J 6 2
♡ K 7 5 4           ┌──────┐            ♡ 9 6 2
◇ K 8 7 4           │ 3NT  │            ◇ J 5
♣ 7 3              └──────┘            ♣ Q J 6 4
                        South
                        ♠ A 3
                        ♡ A 10
                        ◇ 9 6 3
                        ♣ A K 10 9 8 2
```

West	North	East	South
—	—	pass	1 ♣
pass	1 ◇	pass	1 NT
pass	2 ♣*	pass	3 NT
(all pass)			

*checkback Stayman

Meckstroth leads the ♡5. His convention card reads: "3rd or 5th best." Declarer calls low from dummy and the 9 loses to the 10. Perhaps declarer should have played the ♡J or ♡Q to win the trick in dummy. If he had, East could play the deuce to indicate that he could stand the Obvious Shift: spades. But declarer won in hand and now plays the ♣A-K and another club. This is the technically best way to set up clubs, though it doesn't work here. If West held an honor in clubs, declarer would have five club winners.

On the third round of clubs, Meckstroth pitches a heart. This is an important discard, one that we have not mentioned yet in this book. Against notrump, a general principle is that when you pitch from the suit that you originally led, you don't want that suit returned. Some experts play that you can even give suit preference. For example, a low heart here (♡4) says you don't want a spade return and a high one (♡7) says you have something in spades.

Rodwell wins the ♣J and shifts to a low spade. Declarer plays the ♠3 and Meckstroth wins the ♠Q. He returns the ♠5, and Rodwell makes a beautiful duck, not wasting an honor on South's now bare ♠A. How does Rodwell know that declarer is down to the singleton ace? Couldn't West have started with two spades and four hearts to the *ace?*

Declarer plays a fourth round of clubs. Rodwell wins the ♣Q and is able to cash two spades winners for down one.

Rodwell's duck in spades was based on count. He knew his partner began with four hearts, two clubs, and at most four diamonds (else he would have originally led or later discarded a diamond from a five-card suit). So he had to have three spades. Count is an important area of defense, but notice that West did not have to give count — he merely followed suit and East counted.

Which brings us back to one of our main themes. It is absolutely of no importance for West to high-low in clubs to show a doubleton. When he shows out on the third round, East is able to see that it is a doubleton.

Quiz Question: How could West tell East that he holds a spade honor?

Answer: This is easy. West high-lows in clubs, asking for a spade return. Then West throws his lowest heart, saying he does not like hearts — he does not have the ace.

The switch to spades was rather obvious, but notice how much easier it is to defend this hand once your partner has shown a spade honor!

The temperature at Meckwell's table is getting worse because of all the kibitzers. Nearby Denmark is playing against South Africa at a table with no kibitzers. We grab some seats between South and West. Let's take a look. The flag poster has Denmark as North-South.

West dealer
Both sides vulnerable

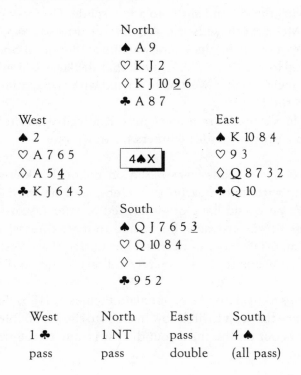

```
                        North
                        ♠ A 9
                        ♡ K J 2
                        ◇ K J 10 9 6
                        ♣ A 8 7
West                                        East
♠ 2                                         ♠ K 10 8 4
♡ A 7 6 5          ┌─────────┐              ♡ 9 3
◇ A 5 4           │  4♠ X   │              ◇ Q 8 7 3 2
♣ K J 6 4 3        └─────────┘              ♣ Q 10
                        South
                        ♠ Q J 7 6 5 3
                        ♡ Q 10 8 4
                        ◇ —
                        ♣ 9 5 2
```

West	North	East	South
1 ♣	1 NT	pass	4 ♠
pass	pass	double	(all pass)

West leads the ◇4. That's interesting. Granted he has no good suit to lead from, but the underlead of an ace is not a recommended lead. Let's see how it works.

Declarer calls the ◇9 from dummy and East plays the ◇Q. South ruffs. No, it was not such a great lead after all. South plays a trump to the ace and the ◇K, pitching a club. West wins the ◇A and switches to a club. Declarer takes the ♣A and plays a high diamond, pitching his last club. Next he plays the ♠9, covered by the 10 and won in hand with the jack. A heart is now led toward the ♡K-J-2, West ducks smoothly and dummy wins the king. Declarer calls for another high diamond from dummy, pitching a heart from his hand. The last diamond in dummy is ruffed in the South hand, and the ♡10 is now led. West starts thinking. Should he go up with the ace or will that crash his partner's queen?

West decides that his partner owns the ♡Q, so he ducks. Declarer overtakes with the ♡J, and ruffs a club in his hand for his 10th trick. As you can see, East-West were entitled to their diamond trick, the ♡A and two spades, so they should have been +200 instead of -790. If West had gone up with the ♡A, he could have defeated the contract by continuing the suit for his partner to ruff or by leading a high club, forcing declarer to ruff and present East with two trump tricks.

It's too bad that the South Africans weren't playing suit preference. How easy the defense would have been, even after that disastrous opening lead. Let's review the play.

At trick one, East's ◊Q was ruffed. Declarer led a trump to the ace and played the ◊K to West's ace. On this trick, East would play the ◊2, showing that he holds a club honor. West switches to clubs (as he actually did in real life). Declarer wins the ♣A and leads a high diamond for a club discard. On this trick, East continues his suit-preference signals by playing his lowest diamond. He continues up the line on the next diamond play. These up-the-line plays absolutely deny a heart honor. South later has no choice but to win his ♡A on the second round of the suit. (He might even win the ♡A on the first round, but then must be careful to return a heart and not a club, which would allow declarer two more ruffs in his hand.)

Quiz Question: Suppose East held both the ♡Q and ♣Q. How could he show both?

Answer: He could show both by following to the ◊K with the ◊2 (we always show honors in partner's suit first), and later he would follow in diamonds with the ◊8 to show his heart honor. It's really easy.

After a nice cold pasta salad during the round-robin break, you wander into the VuGraph room to witness this hand in the match between France and Germany.

VuGraph: France (E-W) vs. Germany (N-S)
South dealer
North-South vulnerable

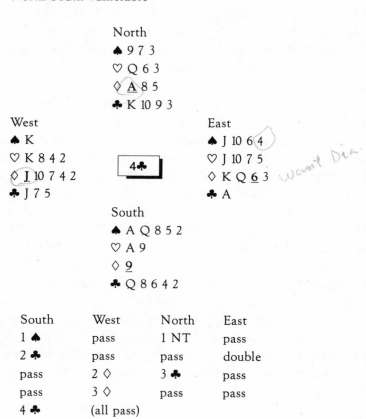

```
                        North
                        ♠ 9 7 3
                        ♡ Q 6 3
                        ◇ A 8 5
                        ♣ K 10 9 3
        West                              East
        ♠ K                               ♠ J 10 6 4
        ♡ K 8 4 2          ┌─────┐        ♡ J 10 7 5
        ◇ J 10 7 4 2       │ 4♣  │        ◇ K Q 6 3
        ♣ J 7 5            └─────┘        ♣ A
                        South
                        ♠ A Q 8 5 2
                        ♡ A 9
                        ◇ 9
                        ♣ Q 8 6 4 2
```

South	West	North	East
1 ♠	pass	1 NT	pass
2 ♣	pass	pass	double
pass	2 ◇	3 ♣	pass
pass	3 ◇	pass	pass
4 ♣	(all pass)		

It's quite a competitive auction, though it appears strange to standard bidders. North would raise spades in American bidding, but the Germans play some sort of system that does not include five-card majors. In any case, the East-West French have pushed the Germans to four clubs, where there is a good chance to defeat them.

West leads a diamond, won in dummy with the ace. Declarer leads a spade to the queen and West's bare king. West thinks for a moment. South has shown a black two-suiter and is probably short in diamonds. The defense better get its heart tricks before they go away on South's spade suit, he thinks. So he shifts to a heart, won by dummy's queen. Not so good.

Now declarer starts the club suit from the dummy, which turns out to be the better hand to lead from. On a low club lead, East wins his ♣A but can now lead back a spade for West to ruff. This will defeat the contract. Unfortunately he plays too quickly and, instead, returns a heart, trying to set up a heart trick. By the way, this East-West pair is on the team that will go on to win this World Championship. So don't think they are slouches. Meanwhile, declarer wins the ♡A, draws trumps and leads a spade to the 9. He is in perfect position to ruff any return, go to dummy in clubs and finesse East in spades. Ten tricks are made.

Quiz Question: At trick one, what was the Obvious Shift and what card should East signal with?

Answer: The Obvious Shift is hearts. Spades is declarer's bid suit. West wants to know only one thing at trick one: Does East have the ♡A?

At trick one East should follow with the ◇6, encouraging in diamonds. East might wish he had a higher diamond spot, but the play of a diamond honor would call for an unusual shift. East doesn't want any shift. He wants West to continue diamonds.

Question: Can East give more help to West after trick one?

Answer: Of course, with a suit-preference signal at trick two. East is able to confirm his anti-heart attitude by following to the first spade with the ♠4, the low spade showing preference for the lower-ranking suit (diamonds).

In with the ♠K, West will return a diamond. Declarer will most likely play a club to the king, and the defense will take two spades, one heart and two clubs, for +200 instead of -130. Even if declarer guesses to lead a club to the 10, East-West will defeat the contract one trick whether East returns a spade for West to ruff or a heart to West's king.

Are you getting the hang of these signals by now? Come, let's look at some more deals. The next one occurred at night while you were enjoying a lavish Italian meal at one of the city's best restaurants. Luckily, however, the next morning's *Daily Bulletin* reports the following hand, from a match between Hong Kong and Brazil.

West dealer
North-South vulnerable

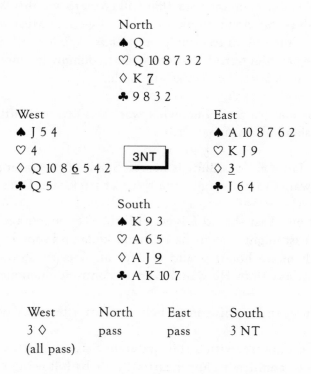

```
                        North
                        ♠ Q
                        ♡ Q 10 8 7 3 2
                        ◇ K 7
                        ♣ 9 8 3 2
West                                      East
♠ J 5 4                                   ♠ A 10 8 7 6 2
♡ 4                    ┌──────┐           ♡ K J 9
◇ Q 10 8 6 5 4 2      │ 3NT │           ◇ 3
♣ Q 5                  └──────┘           ♣ J 6 4
                        South
                        ♠ K 9 3
                        ♡ A 6 5
                        ◇ A J 9
                        ♣ A K 10 7
```

West	North	East	South
3 ◇	pass	pass	3 NT
(all pass)			

Perhaps North should have corrected to four hearts, but he didn't, so the following scenario took place. West led a diamond against three notrump, won by declarer's 9. Declarer played ♡A and a heart. East won and returned . . . a low spade, which allowed declarer to knock out the other heart and make 10 tricks.

The winning play by East at trick four was ♠A and another spade. His low spade play catered to West holding ♠K-9 doubleton precisely rather than ♠J-9 or ♠J-x-x or ♠K-x-x.

Come to think of it, the underlead of the ♠A by East is never right. Even if West holds ♠K-9, he can either dump the ♠K under the ace or win the second round of spades and lead a diamond, killing the entry to the hearts.

Yes, you say to yourself over your morning espresso, East must win the heart and lead the ♠A. It caters to all holdings. Or does it? Suppose South held the ♠K-J-x? South wins the second round of spades and knocks out East's second heart honor. And what if, all along, West held some goodies in clubs, such as the ♣K-10-x? In that case a club shift would have been much better than laying down the ♠A.

Quiz Question: How does East know which black suit to shift to?

Answer: East should have had the necessary information. West is able to show attitude about spades and clubs on the second heart play. He should probably key in on the spades, because that is a more logical shift with a singleton spade honor in dummy.

Holding the ♠K, West will pitch the ♢Q or ♢10; holding the ♠J, West will pitch a middle diamond; holding nothing in spades, West will pitch one of his small diamonds, though he might reserve the deuce for when he holds an especially nice club holding as well.

It's really so simple. On this hand, West should have discarded a middle diamond on the second round of hearts and East would be alert to the idea of cashing the ♠A and continuing spades.

~

You have time for a stroll around town, and at one of the beautiful gardens, you take a break, sit down and read in your *Daily Bulletin* about an oddity: one notrump made one by North-South at one table and the same contract by East-West made at the other table. Hmm, let's have a look. It comes from the Germany vs. Turkey match.

South dealer
Neither side vulnerable

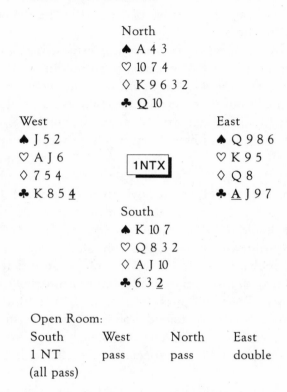

North
♠ A 4 3
♡ 10 7 4
◇ K 9 6 3 2
♣ Q 10

West
♠ J 5 2
♡ A J 6
◇ 7 5 4
♣ K 8 5 4

1NTX

East
♠ Q 9 8 6
♡ K 9 5
◇ Q 8
♣ A J 9 7

South
♠ K 10 7
♡ Q 8 3 2
◇ A J 10
♣ 6 3 2

Open Room:

South	West	North	East
1 NT	pass	pass	double
(all pass)			

In the Open Room, West led the ♣4. Declarer played the queen, East won the ace, cashed the ♣J-9, and switched to a low heart. West won the ♡J, cashed his ♣K, and . . . switched to a spade, for -180. Not so good.

Yet, on a close examination, there doesn't seem to be much room for signaling. East was forced to win the ♣A, and it appears to be right to continue with the ♣J, smothering dummy's 10. West could hardly play anything on this trick but the ♣5, because South might hold the ♣9-x-x-x and West must preserve his ♣K-8 over that.

East's third club play, the ♣9, may have been poorly judged. If it's suit preference, the ♡K is more preferable to show than the ♠Q. So perhaps he should have led back the ♣7. Of course, if he had, West would win the ♣8 (in case South began with ♣9-x-x-x), cash the king, and be faced with the dilemma of having to underlead his ♡A-J-6 to defeat the contract. Would he get it right? He should, because East could have come back the ♣9 from 9-7, but chose to return the 7.

A simpler thought is this. After cashing three clubs, East chose to shift to hearts. Why not shift to the *king*? As long as he is putting all his eggs in one basket, the heart suit, he should make life easy for partner. But then again, what if West held a strong spade holding and only the ♡Q-x-x. A spade shift by East could be crucial.

The real answer to East's defensive problems is this: After winning the ♣Q with the ace at trick one, he should return the ♣7, not the jack. Declarer, with Q-10 opposite the K-x-x, would have stuck in the 10 at trick one. Also, partner would not have led a low club from four little. Once East returns the ♣7 at trick two, West can win and give suit preference on the club return at trick three. The 8 says he prefers spades, the 5 says he likes hearts. When he returns the 5, East wins the 9 and jack, in that order; and, to make life simpler, he returns the ♡K, because he knows for sure now that West likes hearts.

Let's see what happened in the Closed Room.

South	West	North	East
pass	pass	pass	1 ♠
pass	1 NT	(all pass)	

Here West declared in one notrump and North led a diamond. Declarer played the queen from the East hand, and the defense took the first five diamond tricks. North then switched to a heart for -90. Not good at all. Five rounds of a suit were played and the defense still couldn't find a way to cash its other two winners.

Quiz Question: What's the fastest and easiest way for South to tell North that he holds the ♠K?

Answer: Upon winning the ◊A at trick one, he returns the ◊J followed by the ◊10, suit preference for spades. From that point on, the defense cannot go wrong.

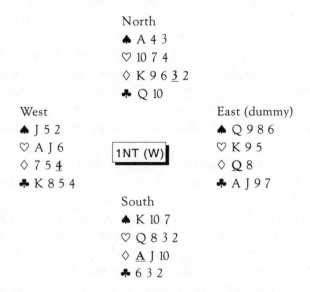

North
♠ A 4 3
♡ 10 7 4
♢ K 9 6 3 2
♣ Q 10

West
♠ J 5 2
♡ A J 6
♢ 7 5 4
♣ K 8 5 4

1NT (W)

East (dummy)
♠ Q 9 8 6
♡ K 9 5
♢ Q 8
♣ A J 9 7

South
♠ K 10 7
♡ Q 8 3 2
♢ A J 10
♣ 6 3 2

Question: Failing that suit-preference play, is there anything else that could have been done by the defenders to let each other know they had two spades to cash?

Answer: Yes, South could pitch a low club to discourage in clubs and a low heart to discourage in hearts. In the meantime, North should cash his last two diamonds by playing high-low. This is suit preference for spades, and when South sees this, he throws the ♡2 and ♣2 to let his partner know that he has help in spades as well. (South doesn't want to squander the ♠10 in case North holds ♠A-J-x.) It's like having a conversation.
North: "I have the ♠A."
South: "That's nice, because I have the king."

~

Today begins the quarterfinal rounds and on VuGraph is a match from the Women's Quarterfinals. You arrive just in time for this deal, where South is in three notrump after East-West have bid and raised hearts. Actually, at three separate tables a heart was led, and all three Souths were allowed to score their games.

North
♠ Q 10 5 4
♡ Q 5
◇ 10 8 5 3
♣ J 9 2

West
♠ J 7 6
♡ 10 7 6 4
◇ K J 9 7
♣ 10 8

East
♠ A 8 3 2
♡ A 9 8 2
◇ 6 4 2
♣ K 5

3NT

South
♠ K 9
♡ K J 3
◇ A Q
♣ A Q 7 6 4 3

In all three cases, after a heart lead by West, dummy's ♡Q was taken by East's ace. East returned a heart to declarer's king, and now ace and a club were played to East's ♣K. A diamond shift by East at this point would defeat the vulnerable game (West can win the ◇K and continue diamonds or revert to hearts, either effectively), but all three East's returned a third round of hearts, giving South time to knock out the ♠A for trick nine.

Quiz Question: How does West tell East to switch to diamonds and not play a third round of hearts?

Answer: This is a hand for suit preference in the club suit and also for a little common sense. When East returns the ♡2 at trick two, South wins the ♡K, and West can surely afford to follow with the ♡10, so that her partner knows where the ♡J is. This is a common-sense play, not a signal.

Whether or not West makes this nice ♡10 play, West can drive the point home by simply giving suit preference in clubs to show where her tricks are. In this case, West goes up the line in clubs, ♣8 and ♣10, to indicate strength in the lower suit, diamonds. East wins the ♣K, and has an easy diamond shift to set up the fifth defensive trick.

Notice, on the last hand, declarer does better by winning the second trick with the ♡K and leading a *low* club at trick three. West's ♣8 will appear high to East, and it will be more difficult for her to find the diamond shift.

~

The next day, Semifinals in the Women's Teams begins. Near the end of the first quarter, you get to watch this deal from the France vs. Austria match.

South dealer
Neither side vulnerable

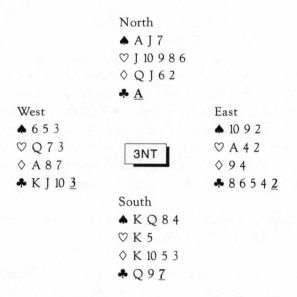

North
♠ A J 7
♡ J 10 9 8 6
◊ Q J 6 2
♣ A

West
♠ 6 5 3
♡ Q 7 3
◊ A 8 7
♣ K J 10 3

3NT

East
♠ 10 9 2
♡ A 4 2
◊ 9 4
♣ 8 6 5 4 2

South
♠ K Q 8 4
♡ K 5
◊ K 10 5 3
♣ Q 9 7

The Austrian South plays in three notrump after opening the bidding one spade and hearing North bid hearts and diamonds. West chooses to lead the ♣3, and East plays the ♣2 under the ace, giving count in their methods. The East-West signaling methods also includes "Smith Echo," so East high-lows in diamonds, when declarer leads them, to show she likes the opening lead. West, in with the ◊A, plays king and another club. South finishes with four spades tricks, three diamonds and two clubs, for +400.

The proper information to be exchanged is this:

1) West leads a club at trick one: "East, do you like clubs?"

2) East plays the deuce at trick one: "Well, I don't want you to lead another one; I have no club honors for you."

3) West holds up his ◊A on the first round of diamonds and wins the second round: "Okay. Where is your entry? I would like to reach your hand to play a club through declarer."

4) East plays up the line in diamonds (◊4-9): "I am telling you. Are you watching my diamond plays?" (*Aside to kibitzer:* "By the way, if declarer had attacked spades, I would have followed down the line, ♠10-9-2 to show hearts.")

Thus, East plays the ♣2 at trick one, attitude. West wins the second diamond, after receiving the ◊4-9 from East, suit preference for hearts. West plays a heart to East's ace and East returns a club.

If declarer puts up the ♣Q, West has an easy time cashing her clubs.

If declarer plays the ♣9, West should work out to cash the clubs anyway. East is sure to be out of high cards, so West can count for declarer four spade tricks, the ♡K, the ♣A and three diamond tricks. If declarer began with ♣Q-9-8-7 and only three diamonds, she has nine tricks without the ♣Q, so cashing the ♣K is still the only hope. But we would bet against the play of the ♣9 from Q-9 doubleton, which would be disastrous if, by chance, East held the ♣K.

Quiz Question: What is the Obvious Shift on this hand and did the ♣2 play at trick one indicate that East had something in the obvious-shift suit?

Answer: The "Obvious Shift," as you will see in Chapter V, is diamonds, the shorter of the two side suits that declarer did not bid. Yes, the ♣2 did indicate something in diamonds, but it was better to lie about diamonds than to lie about clubs, risking a continuation. By trick two, West knew East did not hold a diamond honor.

Sabine Zenkel and Daniele von Arnim have become a top-notch pair for Germany, but they obviously weren't using the Obvious Shift Principle on this hand in their match against Great Britain. As you watch, try to see where the carding error is made.

North dealer
North-South vulnerable

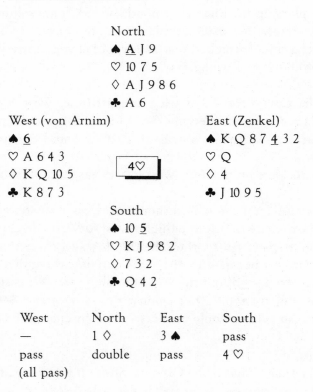

North
♠ A J 9
♡ 10 7 5
◇ A J 9 8 6
♣ A 6

West (von Arnim)
♠ 6
♡ A 6 4 3
◇ K Q 10 5
♣ K 8 7 3

4♡

East (Zenkel)
♠ K Q 8 7 4 3 2
♡ Q
◇ 4
♣ J 10 9 5

South
♠ 10 5
♡ K J 9 8 2
◇ 7 3 2
♣ Q 4 2

West	North	East	South
—	1 ◇	3 ♠	pass
pass	double	pass	4 ♡
(all pass)			

After North's ugly reopening double, South declares four hearts. Von Arnim (West) leads her singleton spade to dummy's ace, Zenkel following with the ♠4 (they play upside-down count and attitude). Declarer plays a heart from dummy, ♡Q, ♡K, and ♡3. Declarer now leads a low diamond. When von Arnim puts up her ◇Q, it is allowed to win. Von Arnim switches to a club (uh oh), which declarer wins in hand. Declarer now plays a diamond to the jack, cashes the ♣A and ◇A, ruffs a diamond in hand and a club in dummy. On dummy's fifth diamond, she throws her second spade. Von Arnim ruffs and cashed her ♡A for the horrible result of -620.

Quiz Question: Von Arnim obviously gave the contract when she switched to a club. How should she have known not to switch?

Answer: Playing the Obvious Shift Principle, East should follow to trick one with an encouraging card, the ♠8 (or ♠2 if using upside-down carding); this says that she cannot stand the Obvious Shift, which, in this case, is clubs. When West wins the ◊Q, she has no choice but to play ace and another trump. Declarer will probably pull the last trump and play a diamond to the jack, hoping for four diamond tricks, to go with four hearts and the two black aces.

East, meanwhile, will be discarding her smallest spades up the line. Having already denied the ♣K or ♣Q, she will show West she has the next-best holding, in case West needs that information.

Actually, declarer can always make this hand if she guesses the diamonds. When West returns ace and a trump, South draws the last trump, pitching a club from dummy, and leads a diamond to the 9. She then exits with a spade. She can ruff a spade return in her hand and finesse the ◊J to run the diamond suit. Of course, this is not a likely line of play, because it is playing East for two singletons. And if this is what she has to do to make her contract, we say: Make her do it! Don't give her the contract on a silver platter. Signal at trick one whether you can stand the Obvious Shift.

~

It's important to remember that defensive agreements are meant to simplify difficult problems. A defender who knows what to do *without relying on a signal* should take charge. This next deal is from the USA vs. Egypt Quarterfinal match. It illustrates a principle that was invented years ago.

North dealer
North-South vulnerable

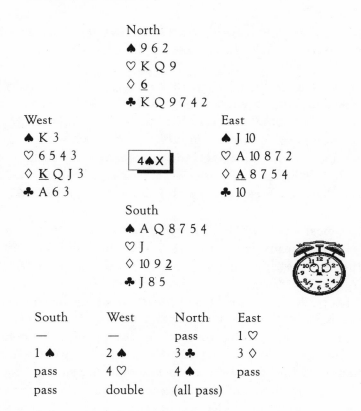

North
♠ 9 6 2
♡ K Q 9
◊ 6
♣ K Q 9 7 4 2

West
♠ K 3
♡ 6 5 4 3
◊ K Q J 3
♣ A 6 3

4♠X

East
♠ J 10
♡ A 10 8 7 2
◊ A 8 7 5 4
♣ 10

South
♠ A Q 8 7 5 4
♡ J
◊ 10 9 2
♣ J 8 5

South	West	North	East
—	—	pass	1 ♡
1 ♠	2 ♠	3 ♣	3 ◊
pass	4 ♡	4 ♠	pass
pass	double	(all pass)	

West leads the ◊K and it is pointless to discuss which diamond spot East should play here. East wants a club ruff and should therefore overtake the diamond and return his ♣10.

In actual play, East allowed the ◊K to win. West shifted to a heart, and East covered the ♡9 with the ♡10. Declarer won his ♡J, and now could have made the contract by ruffing a diamond, ruffing a heart, ruffing a diamond, and playing ace and a spade. However, he took the spade finesse and now, out of desperation, West played ♣A and another club, for +200.

This situation occurs frequently when defenders use their methods as a crutch instead of as an aid. The Principle of Common Sense always gets priority.

The weather in Salsomaggiore is getting very muggy, so you decide to grab a quick cheese sandwich at the bar (and a cold beer) and watch the matches on VuGraph. This next deal is from the Quarterfinal between Israel and the Netherlands. It's amazing how often the defense is unable to take it's top tricks.

South dealer
North-South vulnerable

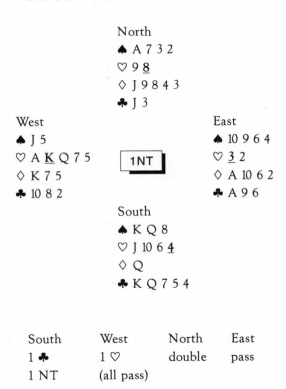

```
                        North
                        ♠ A 7 3 2
                        ♡ 9 8
                        ◊ J 9 8 4 3
                        ♣ J 3
West                                        East
♠ J 5                                       ♠ 10 9 6 4
♡ A K Q 7 5         ┌──────┐                ♡ 3 2
◊ K 7 5            │ 1NT  │                 ◊ A 10 6 2
♣ 10 8 2           └──────┘                 ♣ A 9 6
                        South
                        ♠ K Q 8
                        ♡ J 10 6 4
                        ◊ Q
                        ♣ K Q 7 5 4
```

South	West	North	East
1 ♣	1 ♡	double	pass
1 NT	(all pass)		

The Israeli West leads three top hearts and clears them with a fourth round. South wins and leads a club to the jack and East's ace. East shifts to . . . a spade! Oy vey! The Dutch declarer is allowed to take eight tricks.

Quiz Question: How should West play his hearts to tell East where his entry is?

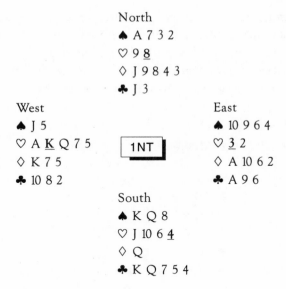

North
♠ A 7 3 2
♡ 9 <u>8</u>
◊ J 9 8 4 3
♣ J 3

West
♠ J 5
♡ A <u>K</u> Q 7 5
◊ K 7 5
♣ 10 8 2

1NT

East
♠ 10 9 6 4
♡ <u>3</u> 2
◊ A 10 6 2
♣ A 9 6

South
♠ K Q 8
♡ J 10 6 <u>4</u>
◊ Q
♣ K Q 7 5 4

Answer: Perhaps West should prepare his plays by leading the ♡K followed by the queen and ace to show an entry in the middle suit. In any case, he must certainly lead the ♡5 on the fourth round to discourage a spade return.

But what if he thinks declarer might attack spades? Then he wants to signal for the higher-ranking minor!

The real answer will come when declarer attacks his suit. Regardless of what West tries to signal by his plays in the heart suit, he can clear this up on the first round of clubs, when he follows with the *deuce* — a loud and clear call for a diamond. And if declarer attacks spades, West can play the jack on the first round, again, to ask for a diamond.

By the way, East follows to the first trick with the ♡3 because he does not want a switch to the Obvious Shift, spades. He is not afraid of West continuing hearts from K-Q-10-x-x, because West would have led the queen from that holding, a popular expert opening-lead agreement.

~

Next up on the big board is the Denmark vs. France Quarterfinal.

North dealer
Both sides vulnerable

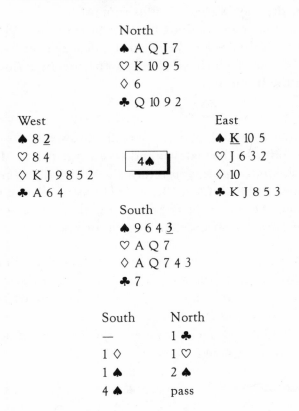

North
♠ A Q J 7
♡ K 10 9 5
◇ 6
♣ Q 10 9 2

West
♠ 8 2
♡ 8 4
◇ K J 9 8 5 2
♣ A 6 4

East
♠ K 10 5
♡ J 6 3 2
◇ 10
♣ K J 8 5 3

South
♠ 9 6 4 3
♡ A Q 7
◇ A Q 7 4 3
♣ 7

South	North
—	1 ♣
1 ◇	1 ♡
1 ♠	2 ♠
4 ♠	pass

West leads the ♠2 to the jack and king. East returns the ♠5, low, 8, queen. The French declarer, a bit desperate for tricks, takes a diamond finesse, losing to West's king. West returns the ◇8 and East ruffs and switches to . . . a *heart*. Declarer now comes to 10 tricks: five trumps, four hearts and one diamond. The defense never scores a club trick!

This one appears to be so simple, we won't even give you a quiz question. West should return the ◇2, suit preference for clubs, and East-West will score the ♠10 and shift to clubs for down one (at least). West, however, might have been afraid that East was signaling with the doubleton ◇10-x. This would not be wise. The ◇10 is an honor in declarer's suit and should not be used so quickly for a signal.

Did you notice any other clue on the last hand that would help East to know his partner held a club entry?

How about the way West played his trumps?

With a heart honor and nothing in clubs, he surely would have started trumps with the ♠8 rather than the deuce. That is, if he were the kind of player who liked to help his partner by giving suit preference in the trump suit.

~

Enough bridge for you? Did that one really throw you? Okay, so you take a day off from the matches and take a side trip to Milan. After a nice shopping spree, you return the next day in time to catch the Women's Final, Great Britain vs. Austria. In the huge VuGraph room, the audience is packed tightly. It is a seesaw match, lots of swings, and a defensive gem or blunder is in the air. . . .

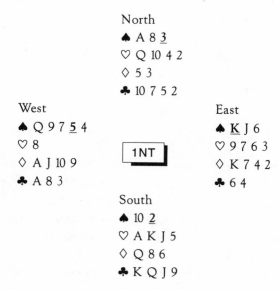

```
                        North
                        ♠ A 8 3
                        ♡ Q 10 4 2
                        ◇ 5 3
                        ♣ 10 7 5 2
West                                        East
♠ Q 9 7 5 4             ┌──────┐           ♠ K J 6
♡ 8                     │ 1NT  │           ♡ 9 7 6 3
◇ A J 10 9              └──────┘           ◇ K 7 4 2
♣ A 8 3                                     ♣ 6 4
                        South
                        ♠ 10 2
                        ♡ A K J 5
                        ◇ Q 8 6
                        ♣ K Q J 9
```

South opens one notrump in both rooms and plays there. Both Wests lead a low spade. The Austrian declarer in the closed room went two down, but the British declarer scores eight tricks!

The British declarer wins the second round of spades with the ♠A and leads a club to her king and West's ace. When West cashes her spades, East plays low hearts and South pitches the ♡5 followed by the ♡K. Now West leads the ◊J . . . but her partner *ducks*. Not best.

Quiz Question: How should West get East to go up with the ◊K?

Answer: West should run her spades in such a way as to deny a heart honor. Let's review the cards. The ♠5 was led to the ♠K; the ♠J returned by East, as West followed with the ♠4. Declarer won this trick with the ♠A and attacked clubs. On the first club play, East should play the ♣4. This is suit preference for diamonds.

Now West wins the ♣A and cashes spades. She must first lead the ♠9 or ♠Q because the ♠8 is still in dummy. She chooses the ♠9, suit preference for diamonds. She continues with the ♠7, followed by the ♠Q, reinforcing the fact she holds diamond strength, the lower ranking of the two remaining suits. In the meantime, East has signaled low cards in hearts and could even play a simple ◊7 to encourage there. When West returns the ◊J, East must know by now to win her ◊K and return the suit.

~

Meanwhile the Open Final has also begun. It turns out that most of the swings at the men's tables are in the bidding. France and the USA are playing a close match and all the players use some form of the obvious-shift method with suit-preference inferences. These pairs — and most great pairs — "make their money on defense." That is, they rarely misdefend.

There was one lone example in the Final, and this highlights one of the drawbacks of detailed carding methods: You must be careful on every single hand! Partner will be paying attention to your cards once you start using these signals.

This was the first board of the fourth set, and perhaps Bob Hamman wasn't quite ready:

West dealer
Neither side vulnerable

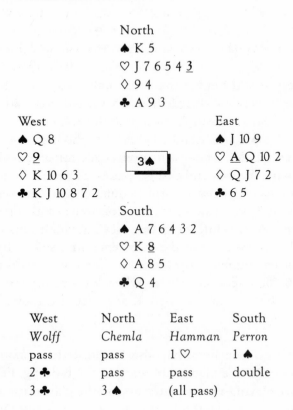

North
♠ K 5
♡ J 7 6 5 4 3
♢ 9 4
♣ A 9 3

West
♠ Q 8
♡ 9
♢ K 10 6 3
♣ K J 10 8 7 2

East
♠ J 10 9
♡ A Q 10 2
♢ Q J 7 2
♣ 6 5

3♠

South
♠ A 7 6 4 3 2
♡ K 8
♢ A 8 5
♣ Q 4

West	North	East	South
Wolff	*Chemla*	*Hamman*	*Perron*
pass	pass	1 ♡	1 ♠
2 ♣	pass	pass	double
3 ♣	3 ♠	(all pass)	

Wolff leads his singleton heart. Hamman wins the ♡A and returns the ♡2, which Wolff ruffs. Was that ♡2 a mistake? No! Here is a case in which suit preference is not available because East has no choice — he must return the deuce or else establish dummy's heart suit. Wolff can also tell that the ♡2 was a forced card, not suit preference, and gets out safely with the ♠Q.

Perron wins the ♠K in dummy, on which Hamman plays the ♠9, and calls for the ♢4. Hamman follows with the ♢2. South plays the ♢5, and Wolff's ♢6 wins the trick. Wolff now succumbs. He switches to the ♣K and Perron wins the ♣A, ruffs his diamond loser and gives up a spade trick for +140.

Wolff thought that the combination of Hamman's ♠9 (if low from ♠J-10-9) and ♢2 promised the ♣Q, and rightfully so. Obviously, Hamman made an uncharacteristic error when he failed to play a diamond honor. However, if he didn't want to play an honor, he could have played the ◊7, steering his partner away from a club shift. Better yet, he should have played the ♠J under the king, a clear suit-preference play in the trump suit. West had bid clubs but had not led them. He was probably dying to know if East had some help for a club switch. If East was alert to this, he would do everything possible to steer his partner away from clubs.

~

The tournament soon ends with France winning the Open Final and Austria the Women's.

You return home on the airplane and, with lots of time on your hands, you review some of the deals, especially those of your favorite pair, Meckwell. Suddenly you spot one that you had missed. Perhaps you were eating a chicken *cacciatore* at a nearby cafe when this one was dealt. But it is a glaring error and you wonder if the Obvious Shift Principle or suit preference could have saved the defense.

The deal is from the quarterfinals, which the Americans won. But on this hand, they misdefended five clubs doubled. Let's see what went wrong.

North dealer
East-West vulnerable

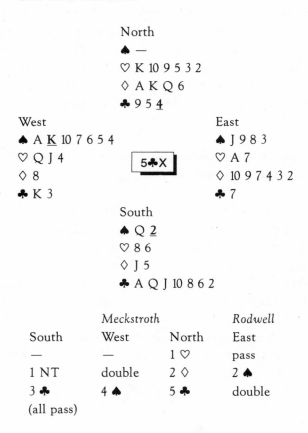

North
♠ —
♡ K 10 9 5 3 2
♢ A K Q 6
♣ 9 5 4

West
♠ A K 10 7 6 5 4
♡ Q J 4
♢ 8
♣ K 3

5♣X

East
♠ J 9 8 3
♡ A 7
♢ 10 9 7 4 3 2
♣ 7

South
♠ Q 2
♡ 8 6
♢ J 5
♣ A Q J 10 8 6 2

	Meckstroth		Rodwell
South	West	North	East
—	—	1 ♡	pass
1 NT	double	2 ♢	2 ♠
3 ♣	4 ♠	5 ♣	double
(all pass)			

In the closed room, the American North-South, Deutsch and Rosenberg, played six clubs down two, for -100. The board rated to be a push. Although declarer here is a level lower, this time he was doubled.

Meckstroth led a high spade, ruffed by declarer. Unfortunately, the hand record does not give East's signal at trick one. The ♣9 was played from dummy, and Meckstroth won the king. Now, however, Meckstroth failed to shift to a heart. He switched to a diamond and declarer scored +550.

Quiz Question: Which spade should East play at trick one to show the ♡A? For that matter, which suit is the Obvious Shift?

Answer: If hearts is the Obvious Shift, East should follow to trick one with the ♠3, saying he can stand a heart shift.

If diamonds is the Obvious Shift, East should follow with the ♠J, an unusual signal calling for the non-obvious shift.

Well, which is it?

The heart suit may produce tricks for the defense and the diamond suit won't, so the heart suit logically is the obvious-shift suit. This means East's correct play is the ♠3, requesting the Obvious Shift.

If, however, you are playing a set of rules which state that the shorter suit is always the Obvious Shift, diamonds would be your pick, and East should follow to trick one with the ♠J, demanding a heart play.

We play that *a suit headed by the A-K-Q can never be the Obvious Shift,* so we would identify hearts as the Obvious Shift.

You may wonder why West needs *any* signal in order to shift to hearts. After all, where else can the defense take tricks? Not so fast.

We believe Meckstroth was fooled by the double of five clubs. He didn't expect partner to double with a singleton trump. He might have thought that Rodwell held the ♣A or at least another small club, in which case declarer will have an impossible time coming to 11 tricks after a diamond return. Notice that Rodwell might have held the ♡A *third* rather than doubleton, in which case the heart shift may backfire by setting up dummy's long suit.

Sometimes an inference from the bidding gets stuck in the mind of a defender and nothing will change his mental picture of the hand. Accurate defense may require accurate bidding as well, and here was an example of such a case.

This book is about defense, not bidding, and the best we can do is try to establish how East can signal where his highcard is. In this case, East-West must determine the Obvious Shift and signal accordingly. On this hand, unfortunately, the Obvious Shift isn't so obvious, and an arbitrary rule had to be applied to keep both defenders on the same track.

There are times when we will need more rules to keep the ship afloat. Let's head to Chapter V and see what we can come up with.

V. When the Obvious Shift Isn't So Obvious

U ntil now, we have discussed the Obvious Shift as if it were reasonably obvious to both partners. We presented a few guidelines for identifying the Obvious Shift in the short quiz at the end of Chapter II. Most important of these was that against a suit contract dummy's weak three-card suit is the top candidate; otherwise we look for dummy's shorter side suit, and if there is doubt, we go with the lower.

On the one hand, these rules are easy, and most of the time you will be on the same wavelength with partner. On the other hand, they do not take into account bidding, which could easily change your thinking. At the table, confusing situations arise. As we saw on the last deal, the Obvious Shift is not always so obvious. And no partnerships enjoy mix-ups.

It is a good idea, therefore, to have a set of firm rules to follow. These rules are valuable, however, only in a partnership and should be treated in the same way you treat bidding systems: You've got to agree on them with partner beforehand.

In our study of defense, both in reading and actual play, we have come upon enough blunders to help us formulate the following set of rules. We have no doubt, however — this being the first attempt at such guidelines — that theorists will come up with even better ideas after these methods become popular. For now, here are our rules, which are designed for accuracy and simplicity.

First we will present five preliminary rules, which say what the Obvious Shift *cannot* be at trick one.

(A) The Obvious Shift cannot be the suit led.
This is because it would not be a shift.

(B) The Obvious Shift is never trumps.
Though trumps may very well be the best shift, it will have to be determined by the opening leader, based on the information he has.

(C) The Obvious Shift is never a suit headed by the A-K-Q or four of the top five honors.

(D) The Obvious Shift in a suit contract is never dummy's singleton or void.
But in a notrump contract it often is.

(E) The Obvious Shift is never a natural suit bid by declarer.
This stands to reason, and by eliminating this suit, you often have the Obvious Shift pinned down. Thus, as we always knew, the more declarer describes his hand, the easier the defense.*

Using these negative rules alone, you can often pinpoint the Obvious Shift. Let's look at one such example, which dates back to 1959! Were experts using obvious-shift carding even then? Apparently yes. The following problem-hand by Alvin Roth and Tobias Stone first appeared in *The Bridge World* and was later reprinted in the book, "For Experts Only."

1959

"Two of the best American players were involved: Ira Rubin, sitting West, and Sam Stayman, North. East was Tobias Stone; South, declarer, was Arthur Seidman, a tough rubber bridge competitor.

---

*Of course, we should never say never. There are times every other suit has been eliminated and only a suit bid by declarer makes sense. But it is extremely rare.

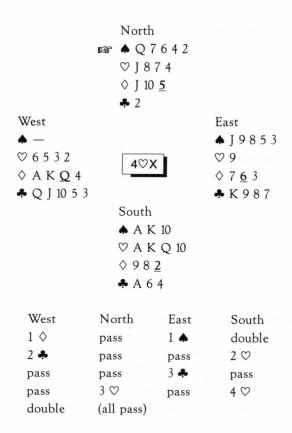

North
☞ ♠ Q 7 6 4 2
♡ J 8 7 4
◇ J 10 <u>5</u>
♣ 2

West
♠ —
♡ 6 5 3 2
◇ A K Q 4
♣ Q J 10 5 3

4♡X

East
♠ J 9 8 5 3
♡ 9
◇ 7 <u>6</u> 3
♣ K 9 8 7

South
♠ A K 10
♡ A K Q 10
◇ 9 8 <u>2</u>
♣ A 6 4

West	North	East	South
1 ◇	pass	1 ♠	double
2 ♣	pass	pass	2 ♡
pass	pass	3 ♣	pass
pass	3 ♡	pass	4 ♡
double	(all pass)		

"Rubin, West, opened the ◇Q. Stone played the ◇6, and declarer played the deuce. Rubin led the ◇K; Stone played the ◇7 and declarer, the 9. Rubin now led the ◇A; Stone played the ◇3 and declarer, the 8.

"In Rubin's position, what do you play now — and why?

"After Rubin cashed the three diamonds, he switched to the ♣Q, and declarer had no trouble making the contract.

"The correct play by West at trick four is a trump, destroying declarer's 'transportation.' Indeed, this trump shift would be equally effective if South had all five missing trumps and only the A-K blank of spades. In either case, needing two club ruffs in dummy, South cannot get back and forth without running into a spade ruff by West. Declarer's dilemma after the trump shift is obvious and we're sure that all readers will easily analyze the situation for themselves."

1994 (35 years later)

Notice East's (Tobias Stone) choice of diamond plays! He followed with the 6, 7, 3. Why did he play the ◇6 at trick one rather than the 3? Because he didn't want a spade shift, the Obvious Shift. West can now play declarer for the ♠A-K. If declarer also holds the ♣A, a trump shift is necessary. If East holds the ♣A, West must consider if the club trick can possibly go away. If not, a trump switch is still in order.

Now for some positive commandments, listed in priority, to determine the Obvious Shift. Examples will follow.

(1) The opening leader's bid suit is the Obvious Shift.

(2) If the opening leader has not bid a suit, the leader's partner's bid suit is the Obvious Shift.

(3) If both defenders have bid suits and the opening leader starts with an unbid suit (which is rare), look at the suits and choose one of them by applying the rules below.

If situation (3) occurs or if no suits are bid by the defenders, apply the following rules.

(4) Against a suit contract, a three-card suit headed by at most one honor (A, K, Q, J or 10) is the Obvious Shift. Against notrump, dummy's shortest suit is the Obvious Shift (even a strong holding such as ace-king doubleton).

(5) When there is no weak three-card suit, the shortest suit is the Obvious Shift. But against a suit contract, this cannot be a singleton or void.

(6) When there are two equal-length suits, either of which might be the Obvious Shift, look at the number of honors. The suit with fewer honors is the Obvious Shift. If the suits have an equal number of honors, the lower-ranking suit is arbitrarily deemed to be the Obvious Shift.

(1) The opening leader's bid suit is the Obvious Shift.

Because he did not lead his own suit, it is probably broken, and he is dying to know if his partner has any help for him.

West dealer
East-West vulnerable

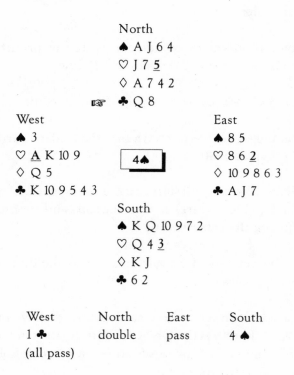

North
♠ A J 6 4
♡ J 7 5
♢ A 7 4 2
☞ ♣ Q 8

West
♠ 3
♡ A K 10 9
♢ Q 5
♣ K 10 9 5 4 3

4♠

East
♠ 8 5
♡ 8 6 2
♢ 10 9 8 6 3
♣ A J 7

South
♠ K Q 10 9 7 2
♡ Q 4 3
♢ K J
♣ 6 2

West	North	East	South
1 ♣	double	pass	4 ♠
(all pass)			

West leads the ♡A (from ace-king). East follows with the ♡2, showing tolerance for his partner's bid suit (clubs). East-West calmly cash two hearts and two clubs. What a disaster it would be for West to try a diamond shift!

Now change the hand slightly. Give declarer ♢x-x and the ♣A-J and give East the ♢K-J-x-x-x and ♣x-x. East plays the ♡6 to trick one. He will follow with the ♡8, showing a non-doubleton heart with no tolerance for a club switch. Regardless of what non-club West plays next, declarer will lose two hearts, one diamond and one club.

(2) If the opening leader has not bid a suit, the leader's partner's bid suit is the Obvious Shift.

You may not always wish to lead your partner's suit. Suppose you hold the king or ace doubleton in partner's suit, for example, with a sequence in another suit. Your partner's bid does not always promise a top honor.

East dealer
Neither side vulnerable

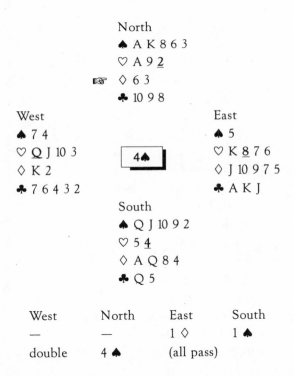

North
♠ A K 8 6 3
♡ A 9 <u>2</u>
☞ ♢ 6 3
♣ 10 9 8

West
♠ 7 4
♡ <u>Q</u> J 10 3
♢ K 2
♣ 7 6 4 3 2

4♠

East
♠ 5
♡ K <u>8</u> 7 6
♢ J 10 9 7 5
♣ A K J

South
♠ Q J 10 9 2
♡ 5 <u>4</u>
♢ A Q 8 4
♣ Q 5

West	North	East	South
—	—	1 ♢	1 ♠
double	4 ♠	(all pass)	

West leads the ♡Q, which is allowed to win the trick. East is fearful about overtaking the heart in case declarer began with the ♡10-x. East simply signals with the ♡8. This means, "Please continue hearts, partner. I do not want you to make the obvious diamond shift. Although I opened the bidding with one diamond, I ask that you continue hearts."

(3) If both defenders have bid suits and the opening leader starts with an unbid suit (which is rare), look at the suits and choose one of them by applying the rules below.

(4) Against a suit contract, a three-card suit headed by at most one honor (A, K, Q, J or 10) is the Obvious Shift. Against notrump, dummy's shortest suit is the Obvious Shift (even a strong holding such as ace-king doubleton).

South dealer
East-West vulnerable

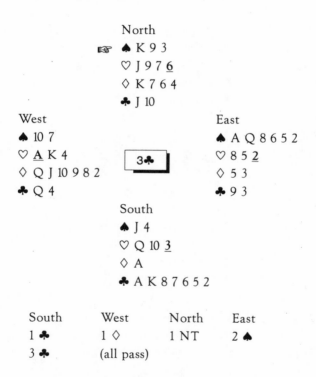

                          North
                    ☞ ♠ K 9 3
                       ♡ J 9 7 <u>6</u>
                       ◇ K 7 6 4
                       ♣ J 10
West   East
♠ 10 7   ♠ A Q 8 6 5 2
♡ <u>A</u> K 4   ┌──────┐   ♡ 8 5 <u>2</u>
◇ Q J 10 9 8 2   │ 3♣ │   ◇ 5 3
♣ Q 4   └──────┘   ♣ 9 3
                          South
                       ♠ J 4
                       ♡ Q 10 <u>3</u>
                       ◇ A
                       ♣ A K 8 7 6 5 2

South	West	North	East
1 ♣	1 ◇	1 NT	2 ♠
3 ♣	(all pass)		

West leads the ♡A. East-West have bid spades and diamonds. Spades is dummy's weak three-card suit, so that is the Obvious Shift. East plays the ♡2 at trick one, asking for the Obvious Shift.

If dummy had three diamonds and four spades, diamonds would be the Obvious Shift. East would have to signal with the ♡5 at trick one (followed by the 8), saying he does not want a diamond shift.

Rule (4) is also the first positive rule to apply when *no* suit has been bid by the defenders. For example:

North dealer
Both sides vulnerable

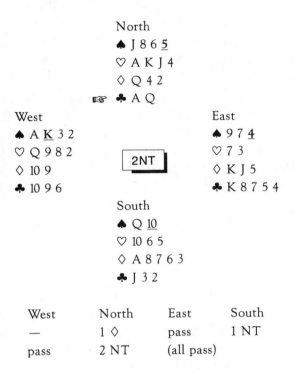

North
♠ J 8 6 <u>5</u>
♡ A K J 4
♢ Q 4 2
☞ ♣ A Q

West
♠ A <u>K</u> 3 2
♡ Q 9 8 2
♢ 10 9
♣ 10 9 6

2NT

East
♠ 9 7 <u>4</u>
♡ 7 3
♢ K J 5
♣ K 8 7 5 4

South
♠ Q <u>10</u>
♡ 10 6 5
♢ A 8 7 6 3
♣ J 3 2

West	North	East	South
—	1 ♢	pass	1 NT
pass	2 NT	(all pass)	

Playing weak notrumps and inverted minors, North opens one diamond and South chooses to bid one notrump.

West leads the ♠K. East plays the ♠4 to ask for a club shift, the Obvious Shift in notrump (shortest suit). Continued club plays will set up three club tricks before South's diamonds are good.

Now suppose the contract was three hearts. (At one table South responded one heart and got raised to three!) The Obvious Shift becomes diamonds. Although diamonds was bid by dummy, it was not bid by declarer and is a three-card suit with only one honor.*

---

*The defenders do not know that declarer has five diamonds.

(5) When there is no weak three-card suit, the shortest suit is the Obvious Shift. But against a suit contract, this cannot be a singleton or void.

This means (to pick an extreme case) that when the two suits are A-K-J third and 5-4-3-2, the three-card suit is still the Obvious Shift. This may not seem logical, but it adheres to the rules, which will keep both defenders on the same wavelength (something that is more important than logic!). You may wish to add more rules to your partnership's understanding, but be careful not to have too many exceptions. In writing our set of rules, we sometimes sacrificed a little logic (as in the case where the A-K-J is the Obvious Shift rather than 5-4-3-2) in order not to get too complex.

We do have a couple exceptions, however. One is that a longer suit is the Obvious Shift when the shorter is headed by the A-K-Q or any four of the top five honors.

South dealer
East-West vulnerable

North
♠ 8 7 6 5
♡ A K Q
☞ ◊ 7 5 4 2
♣ A <u>K</u>

West
♠ A 4
♡ J 10 9 5
◊ A J 8
♣ J 10 9 5

East
♠ 3 2
♡ 8 4 2
◊ Q 10 9
♣ Q <u>8</u> 4 3 2

4♠

South
♠ K Q J 10 9
♡ 7 6 3
◊ K 6 3
♣ 7 <u>6</u>

South	West	North	East
2 ♠	pass	4 ♠	(all pass)

West leads the ♣J. East follows with the ♣8. Declarer next plays a trump to his king and West's ace.

Here is a situation where almost every West in the world would shift to a low diamond. He reasons that declarer has five spade tricks, three hearts and two clubs, for 10, so he has no choice but to play his partner for the ◇K and hope to cash three diamonds.

With our rules, East's signal at trick one couldn't be more explicit. He can't stand a diamond shift, period. West, therefore, must hope that South has done something unorthodox, like bidding two spades on a five-card suit. He returns a non-diamond and the contract is eventually down one.

Now suppose West led the ♡J. The choice is now between diamonds and *clubs*. Clubs becomes the Obvious Shift (dummy's shorter non-singleton suit when there is no weak three-card suit). East follows to the first trick with the ♡2, asking for the Obvious Shift (clubs). West knows that East cannot be in love with the club suit; there is obviously no future there. So he takes East's signal to imply no tolerance for a diamond shift, and he must trust partner.

Finally, we go to rule (6):

(6) When there are two equal-length suits, either of which might be the Obvious Shift, look at the number of honors. The suit with fewer honors is the Obvious Shift. If the suits have an equal number of honors, the lower-ranking suit is arbitrarily deemed to be the Obvious Shift.

For example, A-x-x-x (one honor) is the Obvious Shift rather than J-10-x-x (two honors). If the suits have an equal number of honors, for convenience we deem the lower-ranking suit as the Obvious Shift. Thus, if dummy has side suits of ◇J-10-3-2 and ♣A-K-9-8, suits with an equal number of top honors (ace-through-10), clubs is deemed the Obvious Shift.

~

Let's look at some real-life hands and see how our new rules can help eliminate confusion.

Stockholm Bermuda Bowl 1983
North dealer
North-South vulnerable

                        North
                        ♠ A 7 5 4
                        ♡ 6 5 4
                        ◊ J 10 8 3
                        ♣ K Q

West   East
♠ Q 3   ♠ K 10 9 8 6
♡ A 3   ┌──────┐   ♡ 8 7 2
◊ K Q 6 5 4 2   │ 4♡ │   ◊ —
♣ 9 6 3   └──────┘   ♣ J 10 7 4 2

                        South
                        ♠ J 2
                        ♡ K Q J 10 9
                        ◊ A 9 7
                        ♣ A 8 5

West	North	East	South
—	pass	pass	1 ♡
2 ◊	double	pass	3 ♡
pass	4 ♡	(all pass)	

Italy was allowed to make four hearts against Brazil. West led
the ♣3. Declarer won in dummy and played a trump to the king
and ace. West played a second club to dummy and declarer called
for a low spade away from the ace. East rose with his ♠K and
returned a third club. Declarer drew trumps, cashed the ♠A and
ruffed a spade, then led a low diamond toward the dummy. West,
who held only diamonds, was endplayed for -620.

Quiz Question: What is the Obvious Shift?

Answer: Diamonds, the opening leader's bid suit.

Quiz Question: What should East play at trick one?

Answer: East should play the ♣2, discouraging, asking for the Obvious Shift. On the lead of the first trump from dummy, East should follow with the ♡2, a second cry for a diamond. West wins the ♡A and, rather confidently, shifts to a low diamond. The defense finishes with one spade, one heart, one diamond ruff and one high diamond, for +100.

Stockholm, 1983. On the next hand two world champions could not take their three top tricks against a five-heart contract.

West dealer
East-West vulnerable

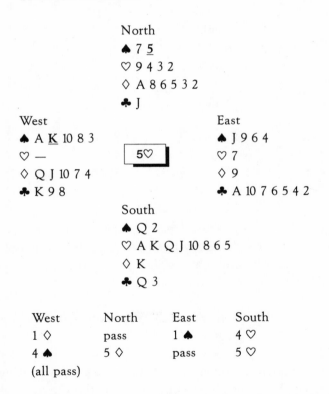

North
♠ 7 5
♡ 9 4 3 2
◇ A 8 6 5 3 2
♣ J

West
♠ A K 10 8 3
♡ —
◇ Q J 10 7 4
♣ K 9 8

5♡

East
♠ J 9 6 4
♡ 7
◇ 9
♣ A 10 7 6 5 4 2

South
♠ Q 2
♡ A K Q J 10 8 6 5
◇ K
♣ Q 3

West	North	East	South
1 ◇	pass	1 ♠	4 ♡
4 ♠	5 ◇	pass	5 ♡
(all pass)			

West's opening bid was a bit esoteric, and he probably meant his pass of five hearts as forcing. Five spades would have been a great spot, but the auction ended with South in five hearts. West led the ♠K. East followed with the ♠4, and West switched to. . .

West dealer
East-West vulnerable

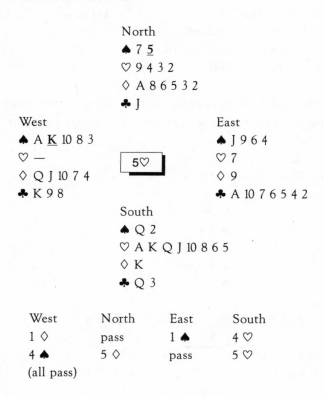

North
♠ 7 <u>5</u>
♡ 9 4 3 2
◇ A 8 6 5 3 2
♣ J

West
♠ A <u>K</u> 10 8 3
♡ —
◇ Q J 10 7 4
♣ K 9 8

5♡

East
♠ J 9 6 4
♡ 7
◇ 9
♣ A 10 7 6 5 4 2

South
♠ Q 2
♡ A K Q J 10 8 6 5
◇ K
♣ Q 3

West	North	East	South
1 ◇	pass	1 ♠	4 ♡
4 ♠	5 ◇	pass	5 ♡
(all pass)			

the ◇Q, for -450. West probably read his partner's low spade as a
count card (declarer followed with the ♠2). In that case, the ♣A
from East wouldn't be enough to defeat the contract, so he tried
to give his partner a diamond ruff.

Quiz Question: How can East tell West not to switch to diamonds?

Answer: For obvious-shift devotees this one's a cinch. Rule (1)
makes life easy. West bid diamonds, so that is the Obvious Shift.
East plays the ♠9, asking for a continuation.

Valkenburg, 1980. In the Australia vs. Ireland round-robin
match, the Irish defenders had no problem defeating this hand:

East dealer
Both sides vulnerable

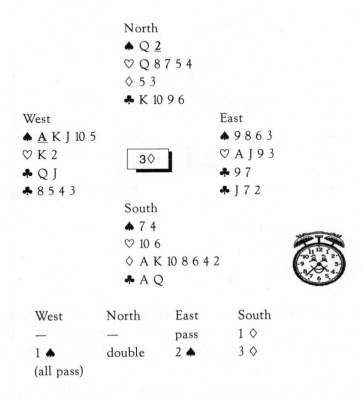

North
♠ Q 2
♡ Q 8 7 5 4
◇ 5 3
♣ K 10 9 6

West
♠ <u>A</u> K J 10 5
♡ K 2
♣ Q J
♣ 8 5 4 3

3◇

East
♠ 9 8 6 3
♡ A J 9 3
♣ 9 7
♣ J 7 2

South
♠ 7 4
♡ 10 6
◇ A K 10 8 6 4 2
♣ A Q

West	North	East	South
—	—	pass	1 ◇
1 ♠	double	2 ♠	3 ◇
(all pass)			

Adam Mesbur (West) cashed two high spades and switched to the ♡K and another heart. East played back a third heart, promoting a trump trick for the Irish side, and East-West went +100.

Quiz Question: What is the Obvious Shift and what cards should East play on the first and second round of spades?

Answer: Clubs, the shorter side suit, is the Obvious Shift when there is no weak three-card suit.

East must follow to the first two spades with the ♠8, then the ♠9. This one-two punch cannot fail to convey the winning information. The ♠8 encourages a continuation and denies tolerance for the Obvious Shift (clubs); and the ♠9 is suit preference for hearts. Easy, right?

South dealer
East-West vulnerable

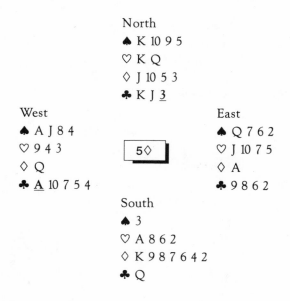

North
♠ K 10 9 5
♡ K Q
◇ J 10 5 3
♣ K J 3

West
♠ A J 8 4
♡ 9 4 3
◇ Q
♣ A 10 7 5 4

5◇

East
♠ Q 7 6 2
♡ J 10 7 5
◇ A
♣ 9 8 6 2

South
♠ 3
♡ A 8 6 2
◇ K 9 8 7 6 4 2
♣ Q

In a quarterfinal match between Italy and Denmark in the Seattle Olympiad, South declared five diamonds after bidding diamonds but not hearts. The Italian West led the ♣A, East discouraged, and West switched to . . . a heart, for -400.

Cash-out situations are very delicate. The Obvious Shift here is hearts, so East must give attitude with hearts in mind. He should play the ♣9 at trick one, encouraging in clubs, discouraging a heart shift. West now places declarer with the ♡A. Since there can be no misguess in spades (West is looking at the ♠J), West has no reason to underlead; he cashes the ♠A and hopes his partner has a trump honor (not the singleton king) for the setting trick.

Quiz Question: If South had bid hearts, what would East play at trick one?

Answer: East would play the ♣2, asking for the Obvious Shift, spades. Remember, once a suit has been bid by declarer, it no longer qualifies as the Obvious Shift. Thus, you must listen closely to the bidding, so you can identify the Obvious Shift in the play.

West dealer
North-South vulnerable

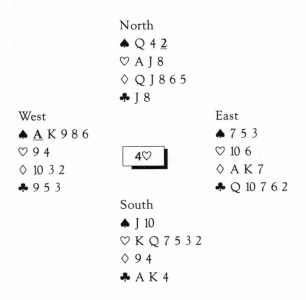

North
♠ Q 4 2
♡ A J 8
◊ Q J 8 6 5
♣ J 8

West
♠ A K 9 8 6
♡ 9 4
◊ 10 3 2
♣ 9 5 3

4♡

East
♠ 7 5 3
♡ 10 6
◊ A K 7
♣ Q 10 7 6 2

South
♠ J 10
♡ K Q 7 5 3 2
◊ 9 4
♣ A K 4

Not only must you listen to your opponents' bidding, you must watch their cards carefully as well. In the Seattle Olympiad, the North-South contract of four hearts was defeated at three out of four tables. At one table, however, North-South were allowed to score +620.

West led a high spade (East following with the 3) and switched to a club — jack, queen and ace. South returned the ♠J. West won, East following with the ♠7, suit preference. But West was not watching the spotcards! He played another club and declarer's second diamond loser went on the ♠Q.

Quiz Question: How would you signal with the East hand?

Answer: Play the ♠5 at trick one, because you don't want a club shift. West will continue spades, thinking that East might have a doubleton. Now East plays the ♠7 and West realizes that East wanted a diamond switch, not a club, which he would have gotten had he signaled with the ♠3 at trick one.

Finally, here is a deal in which one defender thought he was giving suit preference at trick one. The other defender thought his partner was giving count. If only they were on the same wavelength!

The scene of the crime was Geneva. Two world champions were East-West.

South dealer
Neither side vulnerable

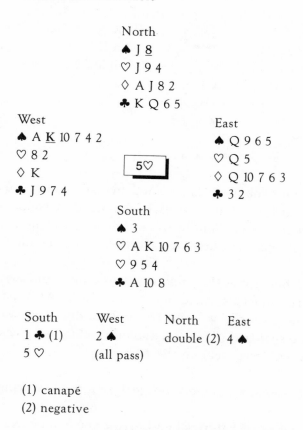

North
♠ J <u>8</u>
♡ J 9 4
◇ A J 8 2
♣ K Q 6 5

West
♠ A <u>K</u> 10 7 4 2
♡ 8 2
◇ K
♣ J 9 7 4

East
♠ Q 9 6 5
♡ Q 5
◇ Q 10 7 6 3
♣ 3 2

5♡

South
♠ 3
♡ A K 10 7 6 3
♡ 9 5 4
♣ A 10 8

South	West	North	East
1 ♣ (1)	2 ♠	double (2)	4 ♠
5 ♡	(all pass)		

(1) canapé
(2) negative

West led the ♠K and East played the ♠9. East-West were using upside-down count signals, and West thought the ♠9 showed an odd number of spades. So West tried to cash another spade. Declarer ruffed, pulled two rounds of trumps and played a diamond. West followed with his king, declarer ducked, and West found himself endplayed! East, meanwhile, meant the ♠9 as suit preference; he thought he had already showed four spades when he leaped to game. Of course, if he wanted to give suit preference, he could have played the ♠Q, a more obvious signal.

Quiz Question: In the methods of this book, what should East play?

Answer: Using obvious-shift signals, East simply plays the ♠5 at trick one, showing tolerance for a diamond shift. South bid clubs and hearts, so diamonds is the Obvious Shift. West dutifully switches to the ◊K. If South ducks, West reverts to spades and declarer will eventually lose a second diamond, for -50.

Remember: We give attitude at trick one.

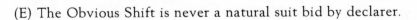

Review

Time for a quick review. Let's look again at the Order of Obvious Shift Suits, beginning with the negatives.

(A) The Obvious Shift cannot be the suit led.

(B) The Obvious Shift is never trumps.

(C) The Obvious Shift is never a suit headed by the A-K-Q or four of the top five honors.

(D) The Obvious Shift in a suit contract is never dummy's singleton or void.

(E) The Obvious Shift is never a natural suit bid by declarer.

Now the positives in order of preference:

(1) The opening leader's bid suit is the Obvious Shift.

(2) If the opening leader has not bid a suit, the leader's partner's bid suit is the Obvious Shift.

(3) If both defenders have bid suits and the opening leader starts with an unbid suit, look at the suits and choose one of them by applying the rules below.

When the defense has bid two suits or when the defense has not bid any suits . . .

(4) Against a suit contract, a three-card suit headed by at most one honor (A, K, Q, J or 10) is the Obvious Shift. Against notrump, dummy's shortest suit is the Obvious Shift (even a strong holding such as ace-king doubleton).

(5) When there is no weak three-card suit, the shortest suit is the Obvious Shift. But against a suit contract, this cannot be a singleton or void.

(6) When there are two equal-length suits, either of which might be the Obvious Shift, look at the number of honors. The suit with fewer honors is the Obvious Shift. If the suits have an equal number of honors, the lower-ranking suit is arbitrarily deemed to be the Obvious Shift.

Stick to the Rules

One day you might come across a choice between K-Q-J third and a four-card suit that looks like 5-4-3-2. For the purpose of staying on the same wavelength, don't change the rules. The "obvious shift" is still the three-card suit. Even if Eddie Kantar comes out with a book of 33 popular exceptions to the Obvious Shift rule, it will still save your partnership countless migraines if you stick to the "simple" rules given in this chapter.

Having said that, let's head to the next chapter, which is filled with aesthetic (and a few esoteric) situations. As you read remember, above all else, the key to defense is to stay on the same wavelength with partner by keeping signals consistent.

VI. Aesthetics

L ife in the world of defensive signaling is filled with surprises. Unfortunately, surprises are the last thing you need on defense, especially when you are in the middle of a crucial deal that may determine a club or tournament championship. In this chapter we will explore some of the more aesthetic situations that come up on defense and try to find some clear rules and understandings to solve similar problems in the future.

When the *Suit Preference* isn't So Obvious

We've just discussed various cases where the Obvious Shift is not always so obvious. We needed special rules to help clarify close situations.

Can confusion occur in suit preference as well?

Unfortunately, yes. When there are three suits to choose from, what do you do? And when there are two suits to choose from, what do you do if you have preference for neither suit?

The answer to the three-suit problem is to eliminate one of the three suits as the least likely switch and choose from the remaining two. Usually you will eliminate the strongest suit. The answer to the second question is to key in on the more important suit and say you don't like it by giving preference for the *other* suit.

These concepts are not simple, but they are crucial when they come up at the table. Our first example deals with the three-suit problem.

Seattle Olympiad, 1984
West dealer
East-West vulnerable

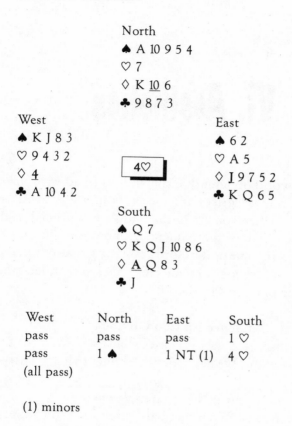

North
♠ A 10 9 5 4
♡ 7
◇ K 10 6
♣ 9 8 7 3

West
♠ K J 8 3
♡ 9 4 3 2
◇ 4
♣ A 10 4 2

4♡

East
♠ 6 2
♡ A 5
◇ J 9 7 5 2
♣ K Q 6 5

South
♠ Q 7
♡ K Q J 10 8 6
◇ A Q 8 3
♣ J

West	North	East	South
pass	pass	pass	1 ♡
pass	1 ♠	1 NT (1)	4 ♡
(all pass)			

(1) minors

West led the ◇4 to the ◇10, ◇J and ◇A. Declarer played a trump to East's ♡A. East returned a low club and the hand was over. Declarer took one spade, five hearts and four diamonds for +420. What went wrong?

Perhaps when West followed to the first heart with the ♡2, East read it as suit preference for clubs. True, West may have led from ◇Q-8-4 or ◇4-3, but the ♣K at trick three is certainly a safer switch and just as good as a low club. When West plays the ♣2 under the king, East can switch back to diamonds and West still gets a spade trick in the end. The best play by East, however, is an immediate diamond return.

Quiz Question: How can East know to return a diamond?

Answer: West should play the ♡9 at trick two as a suit-preference signal: Lead diamonds back, not clubs. (It is dangerous to throw those high trump spots, but a good defender will present his partner with as much help as possible.)

Why doesn't the ♡9 say play a spade?

The logical answer is that a spade play into the A-10-9-5-4 appears fruitless. Here we have three suits to choose from, spades, diamonds and clubs, but only two clear suit-preference plays, the ♡2 and ♡9. *Eliminate one of the three choices.* In this case, spades certainly seems like the suit to cross off.

West plays the ♡9 for the higher-ranking of the two remaining suits. East returns his lowest diamond (his own suit-preference signal) for a two-trick set.

Again, the rule to apply here is this:

Suit Preference With Three Choices
When you have three suits to choose from,
eliminate one (usually the strongest), and give
suit preference for the other two.

Question: Now suppose declarer held the ♠A-Q and dummy's spades were just as weak as the clubs (say, five little). How would West signal for a diamond, when diamonds is not the higher suit or the lower suit, but the middle suit?

Answer: When dummy has no threatening suit, there is no reason to panic. East should return a diamond *regardless of partner's signal* because that is the only suit that may *have to be returned* before the trumps are pulled.

One of the most important questions to ask yourself on defense is: *Is there any reason I must make a shift?* If the answer is no, you should defend passively. A similar question to ask is this:

Is there any suit I must play now or it will be too late?

On the last hand, that suit could be clubs or diamonds, and West tells East by giving suit preference. If dummy's spades were not a threat, the only shift that might be vital is diamonds, and East would return a diamond, regardless of what West signals.

To repeat: Sometimes asking yourself the following two questions will solve a defensive problem without any help from partner.

---

(1) Is there any reason I must make a shift?

(2) Is there any suit I must play now or it will be too late?

Seattle Team Olympiad Final
North dealer
Both sides vulnerable

```
                        North
                        ♠ K 7
                        ♡ J 8 4
                        ◇ 10 8 5 2
                        ♣ K 10 8 7
   West                                         East
   ♠ A                                          ♠ 9 5 3 2
   ♡ Q 7 5 3 2        ┌──────┐                  ♡ K 9
   ◇ J 9             │  4♠  │                   ◇ K Q 7 6 3
   ♣ Q 9 6 4 2       └──────┘                   ♣ 5 3
                        South
                        ♠ Q J 10 8 6 4
                        ♡ A 10 6
                        ◇ A 4
                        ♣ A J
```

West	North	East	South
—	pass	pass	1 ♠
pass	1 NT	pass	3 ♠
pass	4 ♠	(all pass)	

This hand was from the France vs. Poland final in Seattle, won by Poland. West led a low heart to the king and ace. The French declarer played a spade, and West won and found the winning continuation of ♡Q and a heart. East ruffed and played the ◊K. Although the declarer successfully finessed the ♣Q, and cashed a second round of trumps, he was unable to pitch away his losing diamond on the ♣K, because East had a fourth trump with which to ruff.

We would also find this winning defense. On the first round of trumps, East follows with the ♠9. Again, it's difficult to throw high spot cards away in the trump suit, but here's a second example where it's most helpful.

And once again, one suit had to be eliminated from a suit-preference signal. In this case it was clubs, a suit that no defender would want to touch.

Now what if dummy's clubs were also weak. How would West know to continue hearts?

He would know by asking himself the two vital questions.

(1) Is there any reason I must make a shift?

Answer: Maybe. Partner might have started with a singleton or doubleton heart.

(2) Is there any suit I must play now or it will be too late?

Answer: Hearts, so I might as well play it.

~

The next example deals with what to do when you are giving suit preference and you don't like any suit. It was a defensive nightmare from the World Pairs Championship in Geneva, Switzerland. Gabriel Chagas of Brazil, who went on to win the event with Marcelo Branco, was able to fool his Swedish opponents. Let's see what happened:

North dealer
East-West vulnerable

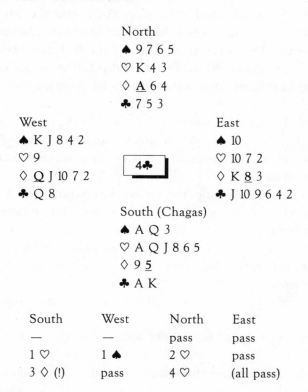

North
♠ 9 7 6 5
♡ K 4 3
◇ A 6 4
♣ 7 5 3

West
♠ K J 8 4 2
♡ 9
◇ Q J 10 7 2
♣ Q 8

4♣

East
♠ 10
♡ 10 7 2
◇ K 8 3
♣ J 10 9 6 4 2

South (Chagas)
♠ A Q 3
♡ A Q J 8 6 5
◇ 9 5
♣ A K

South	West	North	East
—	—	pass	pass
1 ♡	1 ♠	2 ♡	pass
3 ◇ (!)	pass	4 ♡	(all pass)

West led the ◇Q. Chagas won in dummy and played the ♡Q-J, then the ♣A-K, then a heart to the king and a club, ruffed in hand. He next cashed a fifth trump, and West, meanwhile, had to find four discards. Because of Chagas' three-diamond bid, he felt he had to keep three diamonds, so he threw only one diamond and three spades. Chagas was able to set up a second spade trick for a cold top.

A ruse like this should never be successful. East has only one thing to do on this hand, and that is to "scream" to his partner about his spade holding. At trick one he must play the ◇8, which denies anything helpful in spades (the Obvious Shift is partner's suit). Of course, West might think that the ◇8 is a singleton, so the card is not so meaningful.

Here's where suit preference comes to the rescue.

For the rest of the hand, East follows with the smallest cards possible, insisting to his partner that he has absolutely no help in spades. On the first two trumps, he plays the ♡2 and 7, on the ♣A-K he follows with the ♣2 and 4. By then, West should figure out what Chagas had done, especially after South shows up with six hearts and two clubs. East has absolutely denied anything in spades, thus Chagas has at least the ♠A-Q. This leaves room for *at most* three diamonds, which means West can safely pitch a second diamond.

It is sometimes more important to tell partner what you *don't* have than what you do have. We've seen this idea in Obvious Shift trick-one signals. When you can't stand the Obvious Shift, but you don't particularly love the suit led, you often signal a come-on.

On this deal, East holds a singleton in his partner's bid suit, and it is vital that he let his partner know he has no help for him in that suit — more vital than lying about his club-suit strength.

~

Tell Partner About the Crucial Suit as Soon as You Can

On the last deal, East keyed in on the most crucial suit, spades. He gave suit preference for clubs and diamonds, without much strength there, because he wanted to let his partner know that he held nothing in what he judged to be the crucial suit — his partner's bid suit.

On the next hand an Irish pair in the Geneva Pair Olympiad was allowed to make a three-notrump contract with an overtrick. Again, East had to tell West about his holding in West's long suit:

West dealer
East-West vulnerable

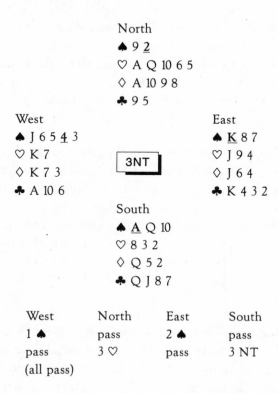

North
♠ 9 <u>2</u>
♡ A Q 10 6 5
◇ A 10 9 8
♣ 9 5

West
♠ J 6 5 <u>4</u> 3
♡ K 7
◇ K 7 3
♣ A 10 6

3NT

East
♠ <u>K</u> 8 7
♡ J 9 4
◇ J 6 4
♣ K 4 3 2

South
♠ <u>A</u> Q 10
♡ 8 3 2
◇ Q 5 2
♣ Q J 8 7

West	North	East	South
1 ♠	pass	2 ♠	pass
pass	3 ♡	pass	3 NT
(all pass)			

West led a low spade to the king and ace. Declarer led a heart to the queen, then ducked a heart to West's king. Nice play! West returned . . . a spade to declarer's 10. Not so nice. Declarer now played the ◇Q to the king and ace, and a diamond to East's jack. East returned a spade and declarer finished +430.

Incredible as it may seem, all East has to do to defeat this contract is follow in hearts with the ♡4 and the ♡9. Let's examine why.

West knew his partner didn't have the ♠Q, but what about the 10? With a second spade honor (the 10 or jack), East would follow in hearts with the 9, then the 4. Thus, the ♡4 at trick two denied the ♠10. When declarer next played a low heart off the dummy, East should give suit preference for the remaining two suits, the ♡J showing a diamond honor and the ♡9 showing a club honor. Here,

East plays the ♡9 and West wins the ♡K and shifts to the ♣6. East wins the ♣K and returns a spade. Declarer will now have to guess the end-position (there is a squeeze endplay against West) to make *eight* tricks.

The Jack as a Low Suit-Preference Signal

In the deal on the next page, a doubled partscore was allowed to make when one defender did not have the signaling tools to warn his partner off a key suit.

There is an interesting sidelight to the hand, with regard to leading a jack for suit preference. Consider the dilemma in the following positions, once shown to us by Michael Rosenberg.

(a)   ♣ 10 x x   (b)   ♣ 9 x x

♣ x   [W E]   ♣ A Q J 9 x   ♣ x   [W E]   ♣ A J 10 8 x

        ♣ K x x x   ♣ K Q x x

West leads his singleton club against a heart contract. East wins the ace and returns an honor. If East has an entry in diamonds, he wants to make a low suit-preference signal. If East has an entry in spades, he wants to make a high signal. But, as you can see, the ♣J is the *low* honor in diagram (a), but the *high* honor in diagram (b).

Our solution to this problem is to designate the jack as a low-suit-preference signal *always*. Let's apply this idea. Suppose East has the ◊A. He returns the ♣J in either case. If East wants a spade return, he leads back the ♣Q in (a) and the ♣10 in (b).

Thus, our rule is:

> The return of the jack is suit preference
> for the lower ranking suit.

Now let's go to our next real-life hand, and see how this applies not only when giving partner a ruff, but whenever you win an ace and return an honor.

A Switch

North dealer
Both sides vulnerable

                              North
                              ♠ 7 5 2
                              ♡ Q 10 7 3
                              ♢ 7 5 3
                              ♣ 7 4 <u>3</u>

West   East
♠ Q 4   ♠ K J 10
♡ K J 6 5   ┌─────────┐   ♡ A 8 4 2
♢ A 10 8 2   │ 2♠X │   ♢ 6 4
♣ 9 8 <u>5</u>   └─────────┘   ♣ <u>A</u> J 10 6

                              South
                              ♠ A 9 8 6 3
                              ♡ 9
                              ♢ K Q J 9
                              ♣ K Q <u>2</u>

South	West	North	East
—	—	pass	1 NT*
double	redouble	pass	pass
2 ♠	pass	pass	double
(all pass)			

*12-14

West led a club to the ace, and a club was returned. Declarer
ducked a spade to East and another club was returned. Next
declarer played the ♢K. West won the ace and returned . . . a
diamond. Declarer played ace and a spade and claimed eight tricks
for +670. (There were four +670s in this final round of the World
Open Pairs Championships. We are not talking about misdefense
at the local duplicate club. Imagine the edge you could have if you
were able to take all your tricks!)

Let's see how the defense should go. Assume West leads a low
club (a high one would be better) to the ace (East would do better
to stick in the ♣10, but, again, let's assume for the moment that he

plays the ace in case West has led from the king). At trick two East returns the ♣10; already East is starting to signal for hearts — if he held nothing in hearts, he must return the ♣J. Declarer wins the ♣K, and plays a trump to East.

East now returns the ♣J and West knows for certain that East has the ♡A, otherwise he would have returned the ♣J at trick two.

You Don't Have to Signal What Partner Already Knows

South dealer
North-South vulnerable

```
                        North
                        ♠ J 4 3
                        ♡ K 9 5
                        ◇ J 8
                        ♣ A Q J 9 8
West                                      East
♠ 8 2                   ┌──────┐          ♠ K 6 5
♡ Q J 10 7             │  4♠  │          ♡ A 8 6 3 2
◇ A 7 6 3              └──────┘          ◇ K 5
♣ 6 5 3                                   ♣ 7 4 2
                        South
                        ♠ A Q 10 9 7
                        ♡ 4
                        ◇ Q 10 9 4 2
                        ♣ K 10
```

South	West	North	East
1 ♠	pass	2 ♣	pass
2 ◇	pass	2 ♡	pass
3 ◇	pass	4 ♠	(all pass)

This one is from the Seattle Team Olympiad. Against four spades, West leads the ♡Q, which wins the first trick. Notice that East could defeat the hand by overtaking the ♡Q with his ace and returning the ◇K and a diamond. We hope we never play against anyone *that* good! So let's assume he fails to find that brilliancy. Is it possible for West, at trick two, to switch to a low diamond?

```
                        North
                        ♠ J 4 3
                        ♡ K 9 5̲
                        ◇ J 8
                        ♣ A Q J 9 8
      West                                   East
      ♠ 8 2                                  ♠ K 6 5
      ♡ Q J 10 7        ┌──────┐             ♡ A 8 6 3 2
      ◇ A 7 6 3         │  4♠  │             ◇ K 5
      ♣ 6 5 3           └──────┘             ♣ 7 4 2
                        South
                        ♠ A Q 10 9 7
                        ♡ 4
                        ◇ Q 10 9 4 2
                        ♣ K 10
```

South	West	North	East
1 ♠	pass	2 ♣	pass
2 ◇	pass	2 ♡	pass
3 ◇	pass	4 ♠	(all pass)

First let's identify the Obvious Shift. The choice is diamonds or clubs. It doesn't make sense to deem a long, strong suit in dummy as the Obvious Shift. Here, however, South has shown five diamonds, and declarer's suit is defined by our rules as *not* the obvious-shift suit. So clubs, despite its strength, becomes the Obvious Shift. An interesting dilemma would arise if the club suit contained *four* honors. By our rules, that would eliminate it as an Obvious Shift. Diamonds would then be the Obvious Shift, because the rules are in a priority order (see p. 95).

On the actual hand, East should follow to trick one with the ♡8: "Don't make the Obvious Shift." When the ♡Q wins (and East knows it will), West will know where the ace is — *he doesn't need East to tell him.** West now must decide whether to play South for

---

*There are those that play count in hearts at trick one, which solves the problem of whether to continue, but does not solve the problem whether to shift to diamonds.

5-2-5-1 or 5-1-5-2 distribution. West should reason that with 5-2-5-1, South might have covered the ♡Q. It is not likely that West has led the ♡Q from the ♡A-Q, but it is certainly possible.

If declarer holds a singleton heart, a diamond underlead will cost only when East has a trump trick and the ◇Q-10 specifically. But in that case, East may very well have followed low in hearts, showing tolerance for clubs, even without the ♣K. He would do this just to keep partner away from a diamond switch.

Interestingly enough, when East plays low in hearts, West, *in no hurry to play on clubs because the declarer's club loser isn't going anywhere*, will probably continue hearts. Thus, we have a weird case: The discouraging low heart gets a continuation and the encouraging high one gets a switch!

The important principle to remember here is that the signal at trick one is not a demand for a play.

> The signal at trick one is informative. West must now use the information his partner has given him to find the best continuation.

Some readers may think this too esoteric, and we don't disagree. In fact, the more we look at this hand, the more it appears that East should, in fact, overtake the first trick and make life simple for partner. Which only goes to prove that a good play is better than a good signal on defense.

Ace-King Confusion

Now let's return to some more prosaic confusion. The Stockholm Bermuda Bowl produced this beauty:

South dealer
East-West vulnerable

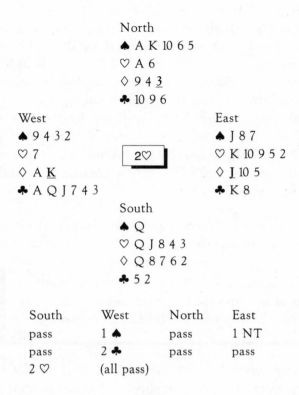

North
♠ A K 10 6 5
♡ A 6
◇ 9 4 <u>3</u>
♣ 10 9 6

West
♠ 9 4 3 2
♡ 7
◇ A <u>K</u>
♣ A Q J 7 4 3

East
♠ J 8 7
♡ K 10 9 5 2
◇ <u>J</u> 10 5
♣ K 8

South
♠ Q
♡ Q J 8 4 3
◇ Q 8 7 6 2
♣ 5 2

South	West	North	East
pass	1 ♠	pass	1 NT
pass	2 ♣	pass	pass
2 ♡	(all pass)		

The bidding was unusual, because East-West were using canapé — shorter suit first. West led the ◇K, normally from K-Q-x, so East played the ◇J at trick one. West continued with the ◇A, showing a doubleton, and East followed with the ◇5. West switched to. . . a spade, and declarer was able to pitch his two clubs away.

East signaled perfectly. At first he thought his partner was leading from the K-Q, so he dropped the jack to show the 10. When West played the ◇A, East now knew West held a doubleton, and signaled with his lower card as suit preference for clubs. West should have read it. Perhaps he did not trust East. If he did, he would switch to a low club at trick three and the contract would be set at least two tricks.

How would East signal if he *didn't* hold the ♣K? He would play the ◇10, just to keep his partner from switching to clubs.

East dealer
East-West vulnerable

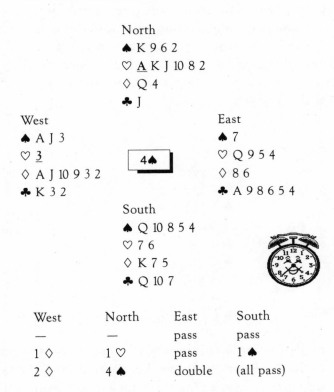

North
♠ K 9 6 2
♡ **A** K J 10 8 2
◊ Q 4
♣ J

West
♠ A J 3
♡ 3
◊ A J 10 9 3 2
♣ K 3 2

4♠

East
♠ 7
♡ Q 9 5 4
◊ 8 6
♣ A 9 8 6 5 4

South
♠ Q 10 8 5 4
♡ 7 6
◊ K 7 5
♣ Q 10 7

West	North	East	South
—	—	pass	pass
1 ◊	1 ♡	pass	1 ♠
2 ◊	4 ♠	double	(all pass)

Here was a successful defense from the Bal Harbour Olympiad. West led his singleton heart. Declarer won and played a trump to his queen. West won the ace and cashed his ◊ A. When East played the 6, West switched to a club. East won and give his partner a heart ruff, for down one. But did the defense really know what it was doing? What if East's diamonds were the ◊ K-6 and he held the ♣ Q instead of the ace?

For years it has been common practice among experts to give suit preference on the first trick if partner's lead appears to be a singleton. Playing Obvious Shift signals, we don't do this.

There are times when you don't know if the lead is a singleton and other times when partner's not sure that you know. East should play the ♡ 9 at trick one: Don't make the Obvious Shift, partner's bid suit (diamonds). West's only hope now is in clubs.

Declaring Against the Obvious Shift

Are there downsides to the Obvious Shift signal? Of course, whenever you give information to partner, smart declarers will also use it. Taking advantage of the defense's information can be a simple matter, such as this deal, described in a confessional-type article by Roselyn Teukolsky in *Bridge Today* magazine.

Roselyn found herself in four hearts against seasoned opponents. West led the ♠A.

<pre>
                    North
                    ♠ J 6
                    ♡ 8 3 2
                    ◇ K Q 5 3
                    ♣ A Q J 10
        ♠A   ♠9
                    South
                    ♠ Q 7 3
                    ♡ A K Q 7 6
                    ◇ A 6 2
                    ♣ 7 5
</pre>

Roselyn: "East contributed the ♠9, whereupon West smoothly switched to the ♣2. I glanced at their convention card, and noted that they lead king from ace-king. Also, they were playing upside-down signals, so the ♠9 was *discouraging*. How should I proceed?"

Roselyn went on to describe her thoughts, none of which keyed in on the important issue: What was East telling West at trick one?

She based her play on percentages. Because the club finesse is more likely to succeed than a 3-3 diamond break, she took the club finesse. Here were the East-West hands:

<pre>
    West   East
    ♠ A 10 5   ♠ K 9 8 4 2
    ♡ J 10 5 4   ♡ 9
    ◇ J 8 4   ◇ 10 9 7
    ♣ 9 6 2   ♣ K 8 4 3
</pre>

Roselyn: "It was only later, during reflection, that I realized that East's discouraging ♠9 at trick one could not have been a falsecard! If he weren't looking at the ♣K, then for all he knew, I might have it. Which means that there was a danger that I might pitch a spade or a diamond loser on the club suit.

"I should have seen that East could not afford to ask for a club switch if he in fact didn't have the ♣K, and therefore it was 100% certain that the finesse *was doomed!* Thus I had nothing to lose by going up with the ♣A and trying for a diamond break later on. My opponents were not being tricky — they were merely defending well!"

Notice East's discouraging spade signal at trick one. *He* wanted a club shift. But West might have thought he wanted a *diamond* shift. Only declarer, who held the ◇A, knew for sure it was clubs East was calling for.

In the methods of this book, the Obvious Shift is diamonds, not clubs. The club suit contains 100 honors, which immediately eliminates it as an Obvious Shift. Therefore, East (playing our methods) would be forced to signal for a spade continuation. This signal would deny the ◇A! West would now have to decide whether to switch to clubs or continue spades.*

As declarer, however, you are not dealing with a world of players who define the Obvious Shift so carefully. Most top notch defenders simply signal discouraging for a shift — any shift — and partner must guess right. Thus, as declarer, your task is simpler, because you often hold the vital information (in your concealed hand), which tells you what East meant by his signal.

~

At the Valkenburg Team Olympiad of 1980, Murray and Kehela of Canada showed their defensive prowess in their round-robin match against Great Britain. But the English declarer might have saved the day had he been more careful:

---

*Frankly, we would not have this problem. We would have led from one of the minor suits with the West hand.

North dealer
Neither side vulnerable

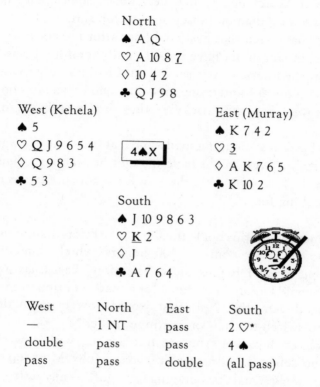

North
♠ A Q
♡ A 10 8 7
♢ 10 4 2
♣ Q J 9 8

West (Kehela)
♠ 5
♡ Q J 9 6 5 4
♢ Q 9 8 3
♣ 5 3

4♠X

East (Murray)
♠ K 7 4 2
♡ 3
♢ A K 7 6 5
♣ K 10 2

South
♠ J 10 9 8 6 3
♡ K 2
♢ J
♣ A 7 6 4

West	North	East	South
—	1 NT	pass	2 ♡*
double	pass	pass	4 ♠
pass	pass	double	(all pass)

*transfer

Sami Kehela led the ♡Q, won by declarer with the king. Next the ♠A-Q were played, Murray ducking. Declarer played the ♣Q, which won, followed by the ♣J. Murray covered this and declarer won his ♣A. On the lead of a third trump, Murray won and underled his ♢A-K to Kehela's queen. Kehela played a heart; Murray ruffed and cashed his high club for a one-trick set, +100.

Could you have defeated this hand, too? Notice the clever duck of the second round of trumps by Murray. He was patiently waiting to get more information from his partner. It was important to discover where Kehela's entry was. It was also important to know that declarer did not hold the doubleton ♢Q, in which case, a simpler defense would be vital.

Kehela discarded a low heart on the second round of trumps and high-lowed in clubs, both times giving the count of the suit. Murray then figured that South held a singleton diamond and was forced into the winning defense of underleading the ace-king.

You could set this hand just as easily, if not more easily, through suit preference. On the second round of trumps, West should pitch the low club — he has no reason to hold on to clubs. Then, on the second round of clubs, West pitches a middle heart (e.g., the ♡6), suggesting something in diamonds, but not necessarily the ace or king. When declarer plays two rounds of clubs, East sees West show out and can place declarer with 6-4 in spades and clubs. This is an even better way of getting the count! If declarer began with a singleton heart and two small diamonds, he surely would have tried to pitch a diamond on the ♡A, while in dummy with the ♠A. Thus if West does not have the ♢Q for an entry, this contract cannot be defeated.

Quiz Question: Could declarer have given himself a better chance?

Answer: Yes. After the ♣Q held, declarer can count 10 tricks if he can draw trumps (five spades, three hearts and two clubs). Since the only thing that can beat him now is a heart ruff, he should attack the only possible entry to the West hand by playing a diamond from dummy. East, with less information, must decide whether to duck. The principle to remember as declarer is this:

> The fewer cards you play before the defense
> must make the vital shift, the better.

On this deal, declarer was giving himself an extra chance by playing a second top club (in case West held doubleton 10), but in doing so he allowed another signal for the defense.

This principle can be extended to many card combinations as well. Often, of course, it is a matter of judgment: Should you sacrifice a technical chance for success in order to gain an advantage in concealment? For example, the following combination was once given to us by our friend Michael Rosenberg:

Declarer (you)		Dummy
♠ A K Q x		♠ J x x
♡ 10 x x		♡ x x x
◇ A K x		◇ x
♣ A x x		♣ K J 10 x x x

You receive a diamond lead against your contract of three notrump. The technically best play is to lay down the ♣A and lead low toward the dummy. Perhaps the more successful play is to lead low to the ♣10 before playing the ace. If the opening leader started with a singleton club, your RHO will win the ♣Q *before he has been given a signal by his partner that it is best to switch to hearts.*

Ethics and the Obvious Shift

East dealer
Both sides vulnerable

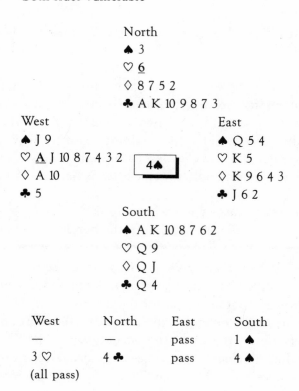

North
♠ 3
♡ <u>6</u>
◇ 8 7 5 2
♣ A K 10 9 8 7 3

West
♠ J 9
♡ <u>A</u> J 10 8 7 4 3 2
◇ A 10
♣ 5

East
♠ Q 5 4
♡ K 5
◇ K 9 6 4 3
♣ J 6 2

South
♠ A K 10 8 7 6 2
♡ Q 9
◇ Q J
♣ Q 4

West	North	East	South
—	—	pass	1 ♠
3 ♡	4 ♣	pass	4 ♠
(all pass)			

The following suit-preference situation arose in Stockholm during the round-robins. At one table five spades went down three, but the other declarer scored +650!

West led the ♡A. East followed with the king! South played the 9. West next played . . . a second heart. Declarer won, pulled two rounds of trumps and ran clubs until East was able to trump in. Declarer lost only the ♡A and ♠Q for plus 650.

East intended his play of the ♡K at trick one as suit preference for diamonds. But West thought it was a singleton, which spelled disaster. There is no perfect way, of course, to signal with the East hand, because East could have been dealt any singleton. But using obvious-shift methods, the king is not dropped, and at least the play of the ♡5 doesn't look as much like a singleton.

If the ♡5 is low, West understands it as a willingness for the Obvious Shift, diamonds. He switches to the ◇A and a diamond, and a third round promotes a second defensive trump trick, for +200.

Quiz Question: When *should* East drop the ♡K at trick one?

Answer: When he doesn't hold the ◇K. He is then screaming for the non-obvious shift. In light of the bidding, it could hardly cost much. In fact, it would be crucial to keep partner away from a diamond switch if declarer held something like this:
♠ A K J 8 7 6 2 ♡ J 9 ◇ K 9 ♣ J 4.
A diamond shift would give declarer his contract.

So where do ethics come in? No matter what East plays at trick one he should do it in tempo. If he ponders over his play, he will be revealing illegally that he holds a choice of plays, and definitely not a singleton.

It is declarer's duty, however, to take at least 10 seconds before he calls a card from dummy — and dummy's duty not to reach for the singleton until the card is called. Otherwise, declarer is putting so much time pressure on East, that East is no longer obligated to play in tempo.

Signaling What You Don't Have

Matchpoints
South dealer
Both sides vulnerable

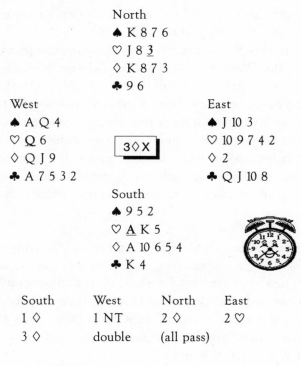

North
♠ K 8 7 6
♡ J 8 <u>3</u>
◇ K 8 7 3
♣ 9 6

West
♠ A Q 4
♡ Q 6
◇ Q J 9
♣ A 7 5 3 2

3 ◇ X

East
♠ J 10 3
♡ 10 9 7 4 2
◇ 2
♣ Q J 10 8

South
♠ 9 5 2
♡ <u>A</u> K 5
◇ A 10 6 5 4
♣ K 4

South	West	North	East
1 ◇	1 NT	2 ◇	2 ♡
3 ◇	double	(all pass)	

Opening lead: ♡Q

Perhaps the most common theme of this book is the importance of signaling to partner that you *don't* have help for him in a key side suit. Keeping partner away from a dangerous shift is just as important as helping him make a vital switch.

This hand was given to us by Eddie Kantar. It was played in a pair event at the 1988 ACBL Nationals in Salt Lake City.

Declarer took the ♡A, cashed the ◇A-K, led a heart to the jack and then a heart to the king. On the third heart winner, West discarded the ♠Q.

Now when declarer led a spade, West was able to rise with the ace, cash his high trump and exit with a spade. Declarer lost two spades and two clubs along with the trump loser.

Yes, if declarer had led a spade or exited with a diamond after cashing only *two* rounds of hearts, the jettison discard would have been avoided and the hand made. Nevertheless, it was a brilliant discard.

Quiz Question: How could East help West to make this jettison play?

Answer: One way for East to help West here would be to pitch the ♣Q on the second round of trumps. West now knows that he cannot shift to clubs! He becomes a desperate man, and must play East for the ♠J.

Question: Suppose East did not hold the ♣10 and therefore could not throw the ♣Q. How else could he help West?

Answer: At trick one East signals with a high heart, saying — once again — he prefers a heart continuation to a club shift (he can stand a club shift only from the ♣K but not from the ♣A). At his next opportunity, East can discard the ♡2, saying he has the next best holding in clubs.

From this point on West must desperately try to avoid being endplayed. Again, his only hope is that East holds the ♠J.

Was Partner's Opening Lead a Singleton?

This is an age-old problem, and there are two solutions for deciphering between a singleton or length lead. Both solutions come from rubber bridge, the training ground of most top players.

One way to find out if partner led a singleton is to play a different suit and see what he signals. If he signals low, it means he held a singleton in his led suit and wants you to give him a ruff. If he plays high, he led from a tripleton.

This solution, of course, is subject to one defender's having the high cards and time to make a play in another suit. For example, look at the following two similar diagrams:

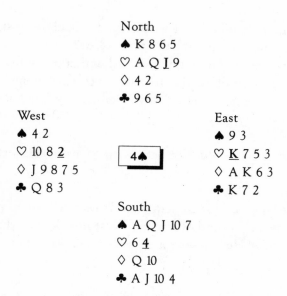

After South opens the bidding one spade, North raises to three spades and South bids game. West leads the ♡2. Declarer finesses and East wins the king. How does East know whether West has a singleton heart? For example, the diagram might be this:

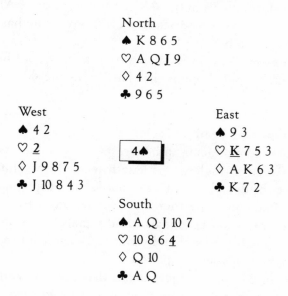

In both cases East should cash the ◊K. On the first diagram,

West signals with the ◇9, saying, please continue diamonds. On the second hand, West plays the ◇5, saying, please switch back to hearts. Both plays in the diamond suit are attitude signals, with the "Obvious Shift" being the suit West led.

The second solution to whether partner led a singleton is illustrated by the following deal from international play.

South dealer
North-South vulnerable

                         North
                         ♠ A 9 6 4 3
                         ♡ Q 10 4 3
                         ◇ K 8
                         ♣ K Q

West   East
♠ J 2   ♠ K Q 10 5
♡ 7   4♣X   ♡ A 8 6 5 2
◇ Q J 10 9 7 6 4   ◇ A 3
♣ 9 6 4   ♣ 8 7

                         South
                         ♠ 8 7
                         ♡ K J 9
                         ◇ 5 2
                         ♣ A J 10 5 3 2

South	West	North	East
pass	pass	1 ♠	pass
1 NT	3 ◇	pass	pass
double	pass	3 ♡	double
3 ♠	pass	pass	double
pass	pass	3 NT	double
4 ♣	double	(all pass)	

How does East know when West is leading a singleton or when he holds ♡J-9-7?

West doubled first, then led the ♡7. That is the clue.

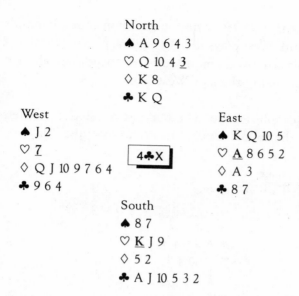

North
♠ A 9 6 4 3
♡ Q 10 4 3
◇ K 8
♣ K Q

West
♠ J 2
♡ 7
◇ Q J 10 9 7 6 4
♣ 9 6 4

4♣X

East
♠ K Q 10 5
♡ A 8 6 5 2
◇ A 3
♣ 8 7

South
♠ 8 7
♡ K J 9
◇ 5 2
♣ A J 10 5 3 2

In real life, East won the ♡A and declarer followed with the king. East shifted to a club and went minus 710 instead of plus 500.

It's really exasperating to be fooled by a baby falsecard. On this deal, East should never have gone wrong. Again, the vital clue is:

When partner doubles a contract and then leads *what might be a singleton*, you should assume it *is* a singleton.

VII. Troubleshooting

The most frequent troubleshooting situation occurs when you have a partner who refuses to learn or has trouble grasping the ideas in this book. There is little you can do about this except to find a new partner or try to work with him until he can name the obvious shift-suit on most defensive hands.

There are two basic technical troubleshooting situations: (1) You don't have the right cards to make the best signal; (2) The Obvious Shift, as defined in this book, appears to be so ludicrous that you don't want to call it the Obvious Shift.

The solution to number (1) is that you should signal in tempo and hope partner can read it. To paraphrase Mahatma Gandhi, an avid bridge player: Bridge is like religion. You are dealt a hand, and you should strive to do your best with the cards *kharma* gave you.

The answer to number (2) is that you should try to do your best with the rules we gave you. If the choice is between K-J-x and A-K doubleton, the doubleton is still the "obvious shift."*

---

*There is a good reason why a strong three-card suit in dummy should not be the defense's first choice for Obvious Shift. When a three-card suit contains more than one honor, it is often dangerous to switch to. Even a *signal* by one defender can be disastrous, because the signal may be more useful to declarer, who might now locate a key queen from the signal.

Here is a list of specific, common, troubleshooting positions, which we will cover in this chapter. They are listed with the page number in case you wish to refer to them after you've adopted these methods.

Troubleshooting Topics   page #

For any additonal troubleshooting, write or fax the authors
of this book through the *Bridge Today* office:
3838 Catalina St, Los Alamitos CA 90702
Please enclose a self-addressed envelope
and allow 4-6 weeks for a response.

On your A-K lead partner shows a doubleton and you don't know which suit to shift to.

One of the exceptions to giving the attitude and Obvious Shift signal at trick one occurs when third hand has a doubleton and partner leads from the ace-king. You must give count if you want to receive a ruff at trick three. But on some hands, when declarer has a doubleton as well, partner will be in a difficult position. He will not know whether you can stand a shift.

One solution to the problem is to play low from the doubleton if you want the Obvious Shift. But you should do this *only if you are certain you don't want a continuation.* For example:

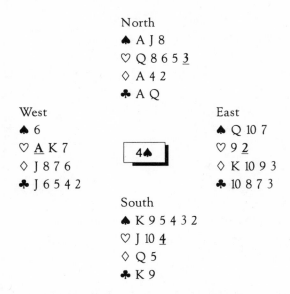

North
♠ A J 8
♡ Q 8 6 5 <u>3</u>
♢ A 4 2
♣ A Q

West
♠ 6
♡ <u>A</u> K 7
♢ J 8 7 6
♣ J 6 5 4 2

East
♠ Q 10 7
♡ 9 <u>2</u>
♢ K 10 9 3
♣ 10 8 7 3

4♠

South
♠ K 9 5 4 3 2
♡ J 10 <u>4</u>
♢ Q 5
♣ K 9

After South opens two spades and North bids four, West leads the ♡A. It can't be right for West to continue hearts and if East signals high, West's winning shift may be a club.

East should signal with the deuce. West switches to a diamond, the Obvious Shift, and the defense takes four tricks.

This deal is a rare bird. The next deal is far more common. East must give count with his doubleton because the third round ruff may be the setting trick.

Unfortunately, West can count the suit, and he knows that declarer also is short. What then does West do when he wants to shift but doesn't know which suit to shift to?

North dealer
Neither side vulnerable

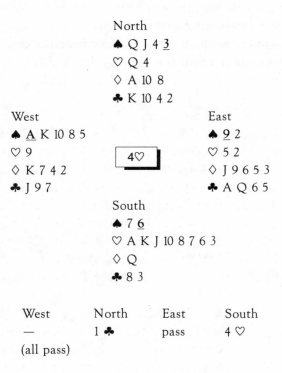

North
♠ Q J 4 3̲
♡ Q 4
◇ A 10 8
♣ K 10 4 2

West
♠ A̲ K 10 8 5
♡ 9
◇ K 7 4 2
♣ J 9 7

East
♠ 9̲ 2
♡ 5 2
◇ J 9 6 5 3
♣ A Q 6 5

4♡

South
♠ 7 6̲
♡ A K J 10 8 7 6 3
◇ Q
♣ 8 3

West	North	East	South
—	1 ♣	pass	4 ♡
(all pass)			

The hand is from the 1993 Bermuda Bowl team final in Chile. Both Norths opened one of a minor and both Souths jumped to four hearts. Both Wests led a high spade, partner gave count and then both Wests considered the situation. The problem for West at trick two is not just whether to continue spades (East might have a singleton), but which minor suit to switch to.

Without looking at all four hands, there are two plausible ways to defeat four hearts after trick one, from West's point of view:

(1) Cash another spade and see if East follows.

   (a) If East has a singleton spade, continue spades and hope East also has the ♣A, which is likely on the bidding.

   (b) If East has a doubleton spade, switch to clubs and hope he has the ♣A-Q.

(2) Switch to diamonds at trick two.

   (a) If East has the ◇Q and ♣A, you may score four tricks.

   (b) If East has nothing in diamonds, but has the ♣A-Q, you get another chance to play clubs when in with the second spade honor.

The player from Norway began with defense (1). He cashed a second high spade, but then switched to . . . a diamond. This was a mistake because even if partner had exactly the ◇Q and ♣A, declarer, with seven hearts to the ace-king, probably has 10 tricks. At the table, declarer went up with the ◇A, led a high spade, East ruffing, and South overruffing. Next two high trumps were cashed, ending in dummy, and a high spade was played for a club discard.

The player from the Netherlands opted for defense (2). Though he might have switched to the ◇K, the low diamond switch still worked, because declarer went up with the ace and relied on the ♣A being onside.

The solution to this type of problem is not always available, but often is. If only one of dummy's two side suits contains an ace, you can try the old-time logic approach — Two chances are better than one.

The Two-Chances Shift Theory
When you don't know which suit to switch to, and you have another entry, switch first to dummy's ace-suit to see partner's signal; then, if necessary, you can switch to the other suit next time.

Partner leads from the A-K and you have three small.

Though we almost always play high from a doubleton when partner leads from the ace-king, we don't always play low from a tripleton — we give an attitude/obvious-shift signal. The difference between a tripleton and a doubleton is that after signaling "high" from a tripleton, you can play a higher spot on the next trick, so partner knows you have three. With a doubleton, once you play low, you can't negate the signal.

In this hand, from the final of the Open Pairs Championship in Geneva, four North-Souths were allowed to make four hearts.

South dealer
Both sides vulnerable

```
                    North
                    ♠ 2
                    ♡ 10 5 4 3 2
                    ◇ A K 10 7
                    ♣ Q 9 5
   West                          East
   ♠ J 10 5                      ♠ Q 6 4
   ♡ A 8        ┌──────┐         ♡ K 7
   ◇ J 9 5      │  4♡  │         ◇ 8 6 4 3 2
   ♣ A K 8 7 2  └──────┘         ♣ J 6 3
                    South
                    ♠ A K 9 8 7 3
                    ♡ Q J 9 6
                    ◇ Q
                    ♣ 10 4
```

South	West	North	East
1 ♠	2 ♣	double*	3 ♣/pass
3 ♡	pass	4 ♡	(all pass)

*negative

After North's negative double, some Easts bid three clubs and others passed. The point is, after West's high club lead, the ♣3 is often considered a forced card. We still play attitude/obvious-shift signaling in this situation.

At the four tables where four hearts was allowed to make (26 times it went down), East-West were playing simple attitude. East played the ♣3 and West switched to a diamond, thinking that East's low club could be from four to the jack and that declarer might hold three small diamonds.

Quiz Question: Is there a way for West to know what to do?

Answer: We recommend that East play the ♣6 at trick one, asking partner to continue. His diamond holding is hopeless, so he knows that even if South ruffs the second round of clubs, the ♣Q won't do declarer any good.

Regardless of what East plays, however, West could utilize the Principle of Common Sense. He needs four tricks to defeat four hearts. What hand with three small diamonds and a singleton club can South have that will allow the four-heart contract to be beaten? No hand. With no highcards in the minors, South would hold strong majors, and the ◇ 10-7 in dummy will be discarded on spade honors. West should try to cash the second round of clubs even if his partner revokes at trick one.

When partner leads from K-Q and dummy has three small or ace third, we give simple attitude.

We're all familiar with the Bath Coup.

On the lead of the king, East must play the 4, even if he has no help in the obvious-shift suit. When declarer ducks, West will know that East either holds no spade honor or desperately wants a switch. This also applies when dummy holds A-x-x and declarer ducks, but does not apply against 10-x-x or J-x-x in dummy.

Crashing trump honors.

Declarer leads a trump and you hold two or three to an honor. If you put up that honor, you may crash with partner's singleton honor. One solution to this embarrassment is for your partner (the one with the singleton honor) to cash that honor, if he is able and smart enough to do so. Another solution is to make a negative inference about partner's signals. When partner *denies* strength in a side suit, he often *holds* strength in the trump suit. A last resort is to ask yourself: What is declarer's trump holding?

West dealer
East-West vulnerable

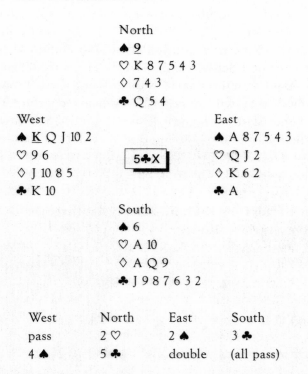

North
♠ <u>9</u>
♡ K 8 7 5 4 3
◇ 7 4 3
♣ Q 5 4

West
♠ <u>K</u> Q J 10 2
♡ 9 6
◇ J 10 8 5
♣ K 10

5♣X

East
♠ A 8 7 5 4 3
♡ Q J 2
◇ K 6 2
♣ A

South
♠ 6
♡ A 10
◇ A Q 9
♣ J 9 8 7 6 3 2

West	North	East	South
pass	2 ♡	2 ♠	3 ♣
4 ♠	5 ♣	double	(all pass)

This deal, from Stockholm, contained a tragic trump situation. And when the crash came, it was not a pretty sight.

West led a high spade and switched to the ◇ J, which ran to the queen. Declarer played a low club and West played . . . the king.

Declarer was now able to set up hearts for a diamond pitch, and he lost only a club and a spade for +550.

Quiz Question: How should West know to duck?

Answer: He couldn't know for sure. But there are subtle clues to the winning duck.

First, what should East signal at trick one? Or should he overtake? Though overtaking could cost if declarer held ♠J-10-x, East must overtake if he does not hold the ◊A or ◊K. Not only is diamonds the Obvious Shift, it is the only conceivable shift, barring a singleton heart in the West hand or a heart void in the East hand.

Then what is the difference between East's low spade signal, high spade signal or unusually high spade signal at trick one?

We suggest that a low spade says make the Obvious Switch, a middle spade says I've got the ♡A as well as a diamond honor and an unusually high spade (in this case, the 8) is a demand for a heart switch (either ♡A-Q or a void). On this deal, East signals with the ♠3 and West switches to a diamond.

In real life, West switched to the ◊J and East ducked. This could have been a disastrous play, because West might have held the ◊A-J-10. East should have gone up with the ◊K. When South wins the ace, West knows the diamond position. Now for the crucial moment. South leads a low club. If West could trust East's trick-one signal of the ♠3, he would know that South holds the ♡A and therefore East holds the ♣A.

Without such a sophisticated signal at trick one, West still has a chance to get the hand right by asking himself: What is declarer's trump holding?

If it is six or more clubs to the ace, he must play the king. If it is seven to the jack, he must duck. With seven or eight clubs to the ace, declarer would surely lead the ace, to catch a singleton king. This leaves the choice between six to the ace and seven to the jack. Because declarer might also have led the ace first with six to the ace, West should probably play low on the club.

We admit, we'd be sweating as West. But in the end, we would have to trust East to have played a high spade if he held the ♡A.

Your entry is in trumps.

Troubleshooting often occurs when your only strength or vital entry is in trumps, a suit that you can't signal for. The only solution to the problem is to keep partner from making a disastrous shift in another suit. This deal is from the Biarritz Pairs Olympiad:*

South dealer
North-South vulnerable

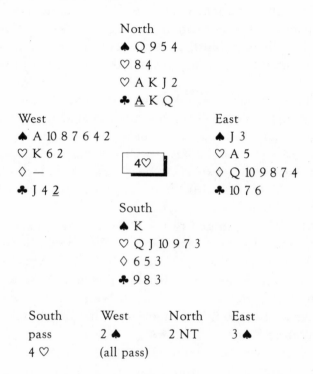

```
                    North
                    ♠ Q 9 5 4
                    ♡ 8 4
                    ♡ A K J 2
                    ♣ A K Q
West                                East
♠ A 10 8 7 6 4 2                    ♠ J 3
♡ K 6 2              ┌──────┐       ♡ A 5
◇ —                 │ 4♡   │       ◇ Q 10 9 8 7 4
♣ J 4 2             └──────┘       ♣ 10 7 6
                    South
                    ♠ K
                    ♡ Q J 10 9 7 3
                    ◇ 6 5 3
                    ♣ 9 8 3
```

South	West	North	East
pass	2 ♠	2 NT	3 ♠
4 ♡	(all pass)		

West led the ♣2 and East followed with the 6. Declarer played a trump to the jack and king, and now West tried to get a diamond ruff by underleading his ♠A. (He probably had the ♠4 stuck behind another spade card.) The result: minus 620.

The Obvious Shift is spades because West bid spades. East must play his ♣10 at trick one to make it clear to partner that he can't stand a spade switch. The defense still needs a diamond ruff to set

---

*Believe it or not, it was played with 14 spades and 12 clubs; there is no error in the diagram. Still the defense should get it right!

the contract. West, forced to play East for the ♡A, should cash the
♠A and continue with the ♠8, suit preference for diamonds.

Relying on a signal when you can do it yourself.

South dealer
Neither side vulnerable

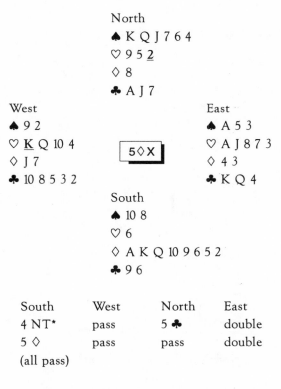

North
♠ K Q J 7 6 4
♡ 9 5 <u>2</u>
◊ 8
♣ A J 7

West
♠ 9 2
♡ <u>K</u> Q 10 4
◊ J 7
♣ 10 8 5 3 2

5◊X

East
♠ A 5 3
♡ A J 8 7 3
◊ 4 3
♣ K Q 4

South
♠ 10 8
♡ 6
◊ A K Q 10 9 6 5 2
♣ 9 6

South	West	North	East
4 NT*	pass	5 ♣	double
5 ◊	pass	pass	double
(all pass)			

*one long minor

On this deal from Biarritz, West led the ♡K, and when it held,
he continued hearts. Perhaps he assumed his partner's ♡3 at trick
one was count from ace-third. Declarer now was able to pull
trumps, knock out the ♠A and dispose of his club loser for +550.

This is a hand where East should take over. Although he
doubled five clubs, he can't bet his life that West will switch to a
club; it is so easy to overtake the heart and switch to the ♣K while
spades are still under control. The lesson is: Do it yourself!

Fooling partner in the suit you lead.

The next troubleshooting area occurs when one defender tries to get the other to make a shift, but in doing so he fools partner in the suit he is playing.

The solution is this: When shifting to a suit, lead low from an honor, even if you want partner to win and shift.

East dealer
North-South vulnerable

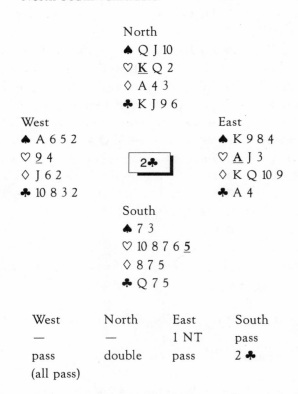

North
♠ Q J 10
♡ <u>K</u> Q 2
♦ A 4 3
♣ K J 9 6

West
♠ A 6 5 2
♡ <u>9</u> 4
♦ J 6 2
♣ 10 8 3 2

2♣

East
♠ K 9 8 4
♡ <u>A</u> J 3
♦ K Q 10 9
♣ A 4

South
♠ 7 3
♡ 10 8 7 6 <u>5</u>
♦ 8 7 5
♣ Q 7 5

West	North	East	South
—	—	1 NT	pass
pass	double	pass	2 ♣
(all pass)			

We don't know what South was doing in two clubs, but that is besides the point. In this deal from the Biarritz Mixed Pairs Olympiad the opening lead of the ♡9 went to the king and ace. East shifted to . . . the ♠8 and West *ducked*. Declarer played another spade. West won and shifted to a diamond. Declarer won the ace, ruffed a spade, cashed the ♡Q and got out with a heart. The defense cashed two diamonds, but eventually had to break clubs for declarer, who got out for down one. Plus 100 was worth 48 matchpoints to East-West, whereas +200 would have been worth 366 matchpoints.

East shifted to the ♠8 in an attempt to discourage partner from winning his ♠A and returning a spade. However, on defense, you cannot create understandings on the spot. West thought the ♠8 was from a doubleton and wanted to save his ace for the next round. Don't confuse discards with leads. When you make a lead, at the beginning or middle of a hand, lead normally, high from a doubleton and low from an honor. Otherwise, you will only confuse your partner.

The principle of leading high to get partner to shift is still a valid one, but it occurs when you want partner to give you a ruff. On this hand, no such possibility exists. If East wants to put West in for a diamond switch, he can do so by leading the ♠4. West is not stupid. He sees that a spade continuation is fruitless.

As we saw on the previous deal, an easier solution is to take over the defense yourself. East could have taken a chance with a diamond switch at trick two. South might hold a doubleton diamond or West might hold the jack. In either case, the diamond shift from East loses nothing.

A similar disaster occurs in the following position, in the middle of the hand, when West wants East on lead to play through declarer in a different suit:

North
♡ Q J 10 9

West   ☐   East
♡ A 8 <u>2</u>   ♡ K 7 6 5 3

South
♡ 4

West must lead the ♡2, not the ♡8, or he will confuse East. The ♡8 must be led only when West does not hold the ace.

Here's another example from international play:

East dealer
East-West vulnerable

North
♠ J 8 7 6
♡ —
◇ Q 9 8 5 4 2
♣ 10 8 3

West
♠ Q 5 4 2
♡ K 10 2
◇ 10 7
♣ K 9 4 2

East
♠ 9 3
♡ A 7 6 5 3
◇ J 6 3
♣ J 6 5

3NT

South
♠ A K 10
♡ Q J 9 8 4
◇ A K
♣ A Q 7

West	North	East	South
—	—	pass	2 ♣
pass	2 ◇	pass	2 NT
pass	3 ♣	pass	3 ♡
pass	3 NT	(all pass)	

South was allowed to score his game after the opening lead of a club to the jack and queen, the ◇A-K, and ♠A-K-10. West won the ♠Q and returned the ♡10 in an effort to get his partner to win the trick and shift to clubs. His partner misread the ♡10, ducking it to declarer's ♡J. Declarer got out with the ♡Q, won by West, who then got out with his last heart. Declarer now had two spades, three hearts, two diamonds and two clubs.

Had East taken his ♡A when his partner shifted to the ♡10 and returned a club, the defense would have taken two clubs, two hearts and the ♠Q. West also could have saved the defense by ducking the ♡Q; declarer had already shown 23 high-card points, so East must hold the ♡A. Still, the entire situation should have been clear as a bell to both defenders.

East's job was to tell West (1) that he didn't have four clubs, so could not stand a second club play and (2) that his entry for a club return through declarer was in hearts. When declarer cashes the ◊A-K, East should follow 6-3, showing heart preference. If he preferred spades, the ◊J would be out of his hand immediately.

West, meanwhile, should follow to everything with his smallest spot cards (◊7 and 10, then ♠2 and 4), indicating further interest in clubs and preference for hearts (over spades). After West gains the lead in spades, West should switch to a small heart. Since he has already indicated he likes clubs, this small heart play is not asking for a heart return. East should have no doubt about which suit to play back.

The solution to all these problems lies in suit preference. Give accurate suit preference and your partner will know when to win the trick, when to continue and when to shift.

Confusion between suit preference and Obvious Shift
Though we have already mentioned this a number of times, it is worth repeating:

> We do *not* give suit preference at trick one.

If both partners would simply stick to this rule, potential disasters could be avoided. If you decide to start making exceptions to this rule, you are going to risk complications and errors.

Here are two examples from tournament play. In the first case the defense went wrong; in the second the defense got it right by applying an exception, but they could have stuck to Obvious Shift methods and had no problem.

Salsomaggiore 1992, Quarterfinals USA vs. Egypt
East dealer
Both sides vulnerable

North
♠ J 8 4 3
♡ A K 3 2
◇ 8 4
♣ K 5 3

West
♠ A Q 9 6
♡ 7
◇ A Q 10 6 2
♣ 8 7 4

East
♠ —
♡ Q 10 9 8 5 4
◇ J 9 7
♣ Q 10 9 6

4♠X

South
♠ K 10 7 5 2
♡ J 6
◇ K 5 3
♣ A J 2

West	North	East	South
—	—	2 ◇*	pass
2 ♡	pass	pass	2 ♠
pass	4 ♠	pass	pass
double	(all pass)		

*Multi, weak in either major

West led a heart to dummy's ace. Declarer played a trump to his king and West's ace. West switched to a club. South won and played a spade. West ducked and won the next spade. Then he switched to . . . ace and another diamond, allowing declarer to ruff his third diamond and claim +790 instead of -500. This was a *big* swing!

The hand should have been over at trick one. When declarer called for the ♡A from dummy, East had a serious problem. If partner held a doubleton heart, he wanted to encourage in hearts. If his partner was leading a singleton (likely because of the double), he wanted to give suit preference for clubs. Readers of this book will no longer have such problems. We *always* signal Obvious Shift at trick one. We *never* give suit preference.

East has only one job on this hand and that is to deny a high honor in diamonds. Thus, he follows suit with the ♡4, indicating tolerance for the Obvious Shift (clubs, dummy's weak three-card suit). On the first trump lead, he gets a chance to give suit preference by pitching the ♡5, again indicating clubs.

On the second trump lead, having seen his partner duck, he can now throw the ◊7 and on the third round of trumps the ◊9. West probably has trouble believing that his partner opened vulnerable without the ◊K, but he has no choice but to trust East, once his partner so violently denies holding a diamond entry.

The next exhibit is from *Bridge Today* magazine's report on the 1989 U.S. Team Trials, by Jan & Chip Martel. (Sep/Oct 1989 issue). According to this book, what should East play at trick one?

North
♠ K 9 6 3
♡ A 3 2
◊ J 9 8 6 5 3
♣ —

♣10

| 5♠X |

East
♠ 10
♡ 10 9 5 4
◊ Q 4
♣ A K J 8 7 4

West	North	East	South
—	—	1 ♣	1 ♠
2 ♠	3 ♣*	5 ♣	pass
pass	5 ♠	pass	pass
double	(all pass)		

*shows diamonds

Opening lead: ♣10, ruffed in dummy

North
♠ K 9 6 <u>3</u>
♡ A 3 2
◇ J 9 8 6 5 3
♣ —

West (Chip)
♠ 8 5 4
♡ K J 8
◇ A K 2
♣ <u>10</u> 9 5 3

East (Lew)
♠ 10
♡ 10 9 5 4
◇ Q 4
♣ A K J 8 7 4

5♠X

South
♠ A Q J 7 2
♡ Q 7 6
◇ 10 7
♣ Q 6 2

West	North	East	South
—	—	1 ♣	1 ♠
2 ♠	3 ♣*	5 ♣	pass
pass	5 ♠	pass	pass
double	(all pass)		

*shows diamonds

Opening lead: ♣10, ruffed in dummy

The Martels: "This hand from the final is a good illustration of the advantage of having firm partnership agreements on defense. When Chip (West) led a club, Lew's (East) play to trick one, the ♣4, was suit preference. Thus when Chip won the diamond lead at trick two (◇ 3, 4, 10, K), he knew that Lew did not have the ♡Q.

"A club tapped the dummy again, and when Lew won the second diamond, he played a heart. . . ."

The contract went down two, but might have made if West had switched to the ♡K after winning the first round of diamonds. The swing difference was 24 imps, so it was crucial for East-West to be on the same wavelength. Martel-Stansby, one of the most practiced partnerships in the world, have more than 100 pages of notes, outlining bidding and defense rules.

The authors of this book have only 10 pages of bridge notes. We find it easier to play when there are as few rules and exceptions as possible. On this deal, Obvious Shift works just as well as suit preference.

Question: What is the Obvious Shift?

Answer: Hearts, dummy's weak three-card suit.

Question: What should East play at trick one?

Answer: The ♣8, encouraging, denying tolerance for a heart shift.

VIII. You're in the Hot Seat

It's time for you to sit in the hot seat. You will defend 20 real hands from world-championship play. Armed with the new defensive machinery, can you now defeat world champs?

Problem 1

North dealer
Neither side vulnerable

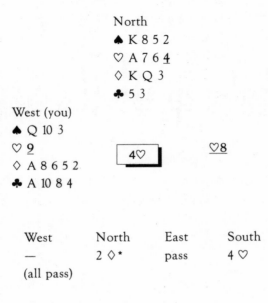

North
♠ K 8 5 2
♡ A 7 6 4
◇ K Q 3
♣ 5 3

West (you)
♠ Q 10 3
♡ 9
◇ A 8 6 5 2
♣ A 10 8 4

4♡   ♡8

West	North	East	South
—	2 ◇*	pass	4 ♡
(all pass)			

*4-4 majors, 12-16 HCP

In the Norway vs USA round-robin match of the 1980 Valkenburg Team Olympiad, Norway was allowed to make four hearts.

You lead your singleton trump to East's ♡8 and South's 10. Declarer plays the ◇4 to the queen, partner playing the 7, and returns to hand with a trump, partner following with the queen, South winning the king. Declarer plays the ◇10. You go up with your ace, partner plays the 9, and you switch to . . .

Solution 1

North
♠ K 8 5 2
♡ A 7 6 <u>4</u>
♢ K Q 3
♣ 5 3

West (you)   East
♠ Q 10 3   ♠ A 6 4
♡ <u>9</u>   [4♡]   ♡ Q <u>8</u>
♢ A 8 6 5 2   ♢ J 9 7
♣ A 10 8 4   ♣ K Q 9 7 6

South
♠ J 9 7
♡ K J <u>10</u> 5 3 2
♢ 10 4
♣ J 2

West	North	East	South
—	2 ◊*	pass	4 ♡
(all pass)			

*4-4 majors, 12-16 HCP

At the table, West shifted to . . . the ♠Q. East captured dummy's king with his ace and then . . . continued spades. Declarer was now in control. He won his ♠J, crossed to the ♡7, pitched his third spade on the ◊K, ruffed a spade, returned to dummy with the ♡6 and pitched one of his losing clubs on dummy's last spade, for ⁺420.

Witnesses say that East-West nearly came to physical blows in the postmortem. West was blaming East for not switching to the ♣K when in with the ♠A and East was blaming West for switching to the ♠Q without the jack. East thought that declarer could have held the ♣A-x-x, in which case it's vital to cash two spade tricks.

If West had shifted to clubs, the defense cashes two clubs and exits with a diamond. They later come to two spade tricks for a two-trick set. Had the American pair been using suit-preference signals, East's up-the-line play in trumps (♡8, then ♡Q) or his up-the-line play in diamonds (◊7, then ◊9) would have indicated a preference for a club shift. Similarly, if West had played the ◊2 on the first round of the suit and discarded the ♣8 on the second round of trumps, East would be certain where the ♣A was.

Problem 2

Valkenburg quarterfinals
West dealer
Neither side vulnerable

North
♠ 10 6
♡ Q 6 3
◊ 9 7 5
♣ K 9 6 5 3

West (you)
♠ J 7
♡ 10 9 8 5
◊ 8 2
♣ Q 10 8 7 4

6♠

◊ 10

West	North	East	South
pass	pass	pass	2 ♣
pass	2 ◊	double	2 ♠
pass	3 ♣	pass	3 ♠
pass	4 ♠	pass	6 ♠
(all pass)			

As West, you dutifully lead the ◊8, to the 9, 10, and jack. Declarer cashes two high trumps, East playing the 2 and 3, and the ◊A-K, East playing the 3 and 4 (while you discard a club).

Declarer exits with a third round of spades. At this point you are down to ♡10-9-8-5 and ♣ Q-10-8-7. You let go of a second club. East wins his trump queen and returns the ◊6, South ruffing. What do you throw?

Solution 2

                         North
                         ♠ 10 6
                         ♡ Q 6 3
                         ◊ 9 7 5
                         ♣ K 9 6 5 3

West (you)   East
♠ J 7   ♠ Q 4 3
♡ 10 9 8 5   ┌──────┐   ♡ J 2
◊ 8 2   │ 6 ♠ │   ◊ Q 10 6 4 3
♣ Q 10 8 7 4   └──────┘   ♣ A J 2

                         South
                         ♠ A K 9 8 5 2
                         ♡ A K 7 4
                         ◊ A K J
                         ♣ —

West	North	East	South
pass	pass	pass	2 ♣
pass	2 ◊	double	2 ♠
pass	3 ♣	pass	3 ♠
pass	4 ♠	pass	6 ♠
(all pass)			

If you got this one wrong, reread Chapter III on suit preference.
  In the quarterfinals of the world championships, two different
Wests pitched a heart, allowing declarer to score a small slam in
spades.

Notice how clever South was not to bid his heart suit! Still, to
pitch a heart after all the signals West received from partner is a
travesty.

After playing the ◊ 10 at trick one, East followed with the ♠ 3
and ♠ 4, the ◊ 3 and ◊ 4, etc., etc. This is "screaming" for clubs, and
the whole hand is a readout. West should painlessly pitch a third
club . . . and a fourth and fifth club on the final two trumps!

Problem 3

Geneva Rosenblum Cup Team final, America vs. Germany. You are West on this crucial deal:

South dealer
Both sides vulnerable

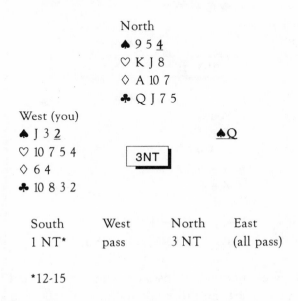

North
♠ 9 5 <u>4</u>
♡ K J 8
◇ A 10 7
♣ Q J 7 5

West (you)
♠ J 3 <u>2</u>
♡ 10 7 5 4
◇ 6 4
♣ 10 8 3 2

♠Q

| 3NT |

South	West	North	East
1 NT*	pass	3 NT	(all pass)

*12-15

You choose to lead a low spade to the queen and ace. Declarer plays the ◇2 to the ace, partner playing the ◇3. Declarer calls for the ◇10 from dummy, partner plays the ◇5 and declarer the ◇8. Next declarer plays the ♡J from dummy, 2, 3, 4. He crosses to his hand with a diamond to the king, East playing the jack, while you discard a club.

Declarer now plays a club to the jack and East's king. East returns the ♠6. Declarer goes up with the king, and you . . .

Solution 3

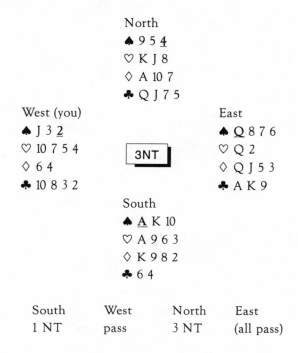

North
♠ 9 5 <u>4</u>
♡ K J 8
◇ A 10 7
♣ Q J 7 5

West (you)
♠ J 3 <u>2</u>
♡ 10 7 5 4
◇ 6 4
♣ 10 8 3 2

East
♠ <u>Q</u> 8 7 6
♡ Q 2
◇ Q J 5 3
♣ A K 9

3NT

South
♠ <u>A</u> K 10
♡ A 9 6 3
◇ K 9 8 2
♣ 6 4

South	West	North	East
1 NT	pass	3 NT	(all pass)

At the table West unblocked his jack! Declarer finished with three spades, three hearts and three diamonds, for ⁺600 and a big game swing.

How could West know who had the ♠10?

East, having denied the ♠J at trick one, must give suit preference about the 10. When he played the ◇3 followed by the ◇5, he was indicating that he had no further interest in spades. Therefore, West should know to keep his ♠J. (If East chooses to cover the ◇10. he should do so with the jack, not the queen.)

Perhaps East should return the ♠8 to make it easier for West. This may be, but another time it will fool West on the spade count. Having signaled violently for clubs, East's ♠6 return should not have caused a problem.

Another clue for West was provided by declarer, who went to dummy to lead the ♡J. It appears he was going out of his way to keep East off lead. Why? The only answer that makes sense is that he holds a spade tenace.

Problem 4

Stockholm Bermuda Bowl
North dealer
North-South vulnerable

North
♠ <u>A</u> Q 10 9
♡ 5
◇ 7 6 3
♣ K J 6 4 2

♠ 3

East (you)
♠ K J 8 7 6 4 <u>2</u>
♡ A 8
◇ 10
♣ A Q 3

5 ◇ X

West	North	East	South
—	pass	1 ♠	2 ◇
3 ♡*	pass	3 ♠	pass
pass	4 ◇	4 ♡	5 ◇
pass	pass	double	(all pass)

*weak

Partner leads the ♠3. Declarer wins the ♠A, following with the 5, and plays a heart. You grab your ace, ♡2 from declarer, queen from partner. What next?

Solution 4

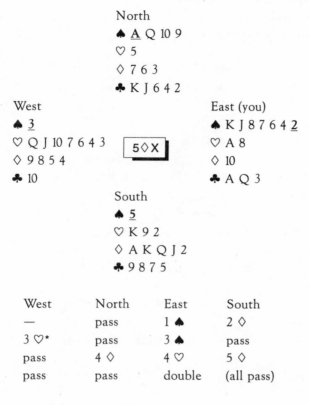

North
♠ <u>A</u> Q 10 9
♡ 5
◇ 7 6 3
♣ K J 6 4 2

West
♠ <u>3</u>
♡ Q J 10 7 6 4 3
◇ 9 8 5 4
♣ 10

5◇X

East (you)
♠ K J 8 7 6 4 <u>2</u>
♡ A 8
◇ 10
♣ A Q 3

South
♠ <u>5</u>
♡ K 9 2
◇ A K Q J 2
♣ 9 8 7 5

West	North	East	South
—	pass	1 ♠	2 ◇
3 ♡*	pass	3 ♠	pass
pass	4 ◇	4 ♡	5 ◇
pass	pass	double	(all pass)

*weak

Return the ♠4. This will lead to ⁺500, at the very least. Does this seem too easy?

Partner could not have been more clear about his request for a spade return. Yet in actual international competition, where two tables declared this contract, one declarer went off only one (East rose with his ♡A and returned a heart) and the other declarer scored his game when East ducked his ♡A and later misdefended. We don't want to name the players and embarrass these Easts, but you should know that they are both world champions!

Problem 5

Bal Harbour, World Olympiad Pairs 1986
East dealer
Both sides vulnerable

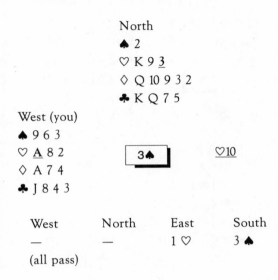

North
♠ 2
♡ K 9 3
♢ Q 10 9 3 2
♣ K Q 7 5

West (you)
♠ 9 6 3
♡ A 8 2
♢ A 7 4
♣ J 8 4 3

3♠   ♡10

West	North	East	South
—	—	1 ♡	3 ♠
(all pass)			

You lead the ♡A and partner plays the 10. What now?

This hand is noteworthy because Meckstroth-Rodwell and Compton-Wold, two leading contenders in the 1986 World Olympiad Pairs Championship, were unable to defeat three spades. (Meckwell went on to win.)

Solution 5

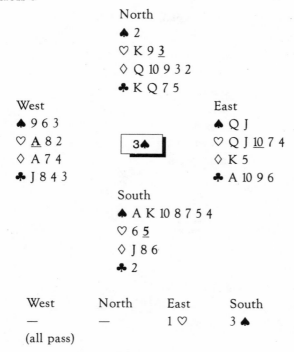

North
- ♠ 2
- ♡ K 9 3
- ◇ Q 10 9 3 2
- ♣ K Q 7 5

West
- ♠ 9 6 3
- ♡ A 8 2
- ◇ A 7 4
- ♣ J 8 4 3

3♠

East
- ♠ Q J
- ♡ Q J 10 7 4
- ◇ K 5
- ♣ A 10 9 6

South
- ♠ A K 10 8 7 5 4
- ♡ 6 5
- ◇ J 8 6
- ♣ 2

West	North	East	South
—	—	1 ♡	3 ♠

(all pass)

Switch to a low diamond. South has at most a doubleton heart, so a heart continuation is fruitless. East is not asking for a club switch, which he could do with a discouraging heart. No, it appears that East has ◇K or ◇K-J or maybe a doubleton diamond with the ♠A. In any of these cases, a low diamond is the winner.

East wins his ◇K and returns a diamond. The third round of diamonds is ruffed by East, who returns the ♡J in case South holds three hearts and a club void. Eventually East must score his ♣A for down one.

East's ♡10 did not demand a diamond switch. It merely said he could stand the Obvious Shift *if it looked good to West*. If West started with the ◇J-x-x or ◇x-x-x, it would be silly to shift to a diamond. If East wanted to, he could have "screamed" for a diamond by following to the first trick with a higher honor. For example, with the ◇A-K and nothing in clubs, East follows to trick one with the ♡J, demanding the non-obvious shift.

Good defense often requires cooperation between defenders.

East cannot signal low at trick one, because if West switches to a club and East wins the ace, East still has no idea whether West holds the ♢A; he won't know whether to lay down the ♢K. This is why East should indicate *tolerance* for a diamond shift, putting the ball in West's court. "I have something in diamonds; do you?"

Problem 6a

Bal Harbour Olympiad
East dealer
Neither side vulnerable

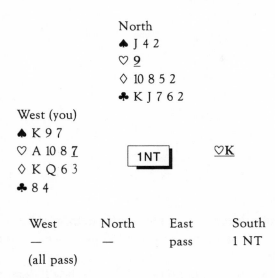

North
♠ J 4 2
♡ 9
♢ 10 8 5 2
♣ K J 7 6 2

West (you)
♠ K 9 7
♡ A 10 8 7
♢ K Q 6 3
♣ 8 4

| 1NT |

♡K

West	North	East	South
—	—	pass	1 NT
(all pass)			

You lead the ♡7. Partner wins the king as declarer follows with the ♡3. Partner returns the ♡J, to South's queen and your ace, while a spade is thrown from dummy. In which order to you cash your hearts?

Solution 6a

Play the 8-10, suit preference for diamonds over spades (you could hardly want clubs). Partner follows with the ♡2-4 and declarer with the ♡5-6 as dummy pitches two more spades.

Problem 6b

What do you play to trick five?

Solution 6b

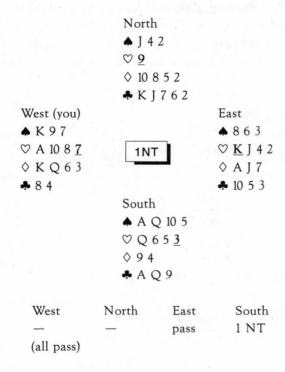

North
♠ J 4 2
♡ **9**
◇ 10 8 5 2
♣ K J 7 6 2

West (you)
♠ K 9 7
♡ A 10 8 **7**
◇ K Q 6 3
♣ 8 4

1NT

East
♠ 8 6 3
♡ **K** J 4 2
◇ A J 7
♣ 10 5 3

South
♠ A Q 10 5
♡ Q 6 5 **3**
◇ 9 4
♣ A Q 9

West	North	East	South
—	—	pass	1 NT
(all pass)			

Partner certainly doesn't have any spade help, else he would have continued playing hearts "down-the-line." Does he prefer diamonds or clubs?

As it happens, either a diamond or a club switch will defeat this contract. The vital switch *to avoid* is spades.

Problem 7

Bal Harbour Olympiad Pairs
North dealer
East-West vulnerable

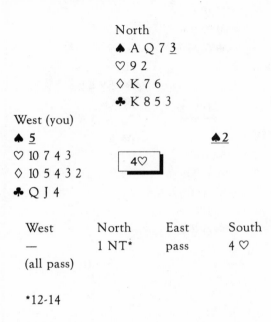

North
♠ A Q 7 3
♡ 9 2
◇ K 7 6
♣ K 8 5 3

West (you)
♠ 5   ♠ 2
♡ 10 7 4 3
◇ 10 5 4 3 2   4♡
♣ Q J 4

West	North	East	South
—	1 NT*	pass	4 ♡
(all pass)			

*12-14

You lead your singleton spade. Declarer wins partner's ♠2 with the 10. He next plays the ♠K. You ruff and partner follows with the ♠J. Your play.

Solution 7

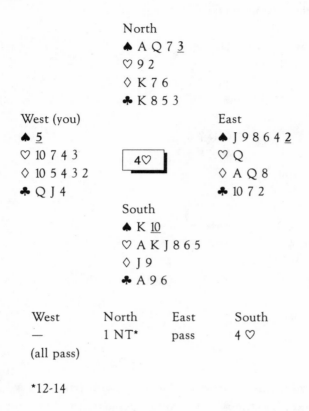

North
♠ A Q 7 <u>3</u>
♡ 9 2
◇ K 7 6
♣ K 8 5 3

West (you)
♠ <u>5</u>
♡ 10 7 4 3
◇ 10 5 4 3 2
♣ Q J 4

East
♠ J 9 8 6 4 <u>2</u>
♡ Q
◇ A Q 8
♣ 10 7 2

4♡

South
♠ K <u>10</u>
♡ A K J 8 6 5
◇ J 9
♣ A 9 6

West	North	East	South
—	1 NT*	pass	4 ♡
(all pass)			

*12-14

This is easy. Partner's first play was discouraging, saying he could stand the Obvious Shift, diamonds. Partner next gave a clear suit preference for diamonds, the higher ranking of dummy's minor suits. You should switch to the ◇5 to avoid any confusion (a low diamond return would indicate an honor and partner would stick in the jack from ace-jack if declarer called low from dummy).

Partner cashes the ◇A-Q and plays back another spade, which creates a second defensive trump trick, for down one.

Problem 8

Bal Harbour Women's Pairs (here's your chance, guys)

Amalya Kearse and Jacqui Mitchell won the World Women's Pairs in Bal Harbour. On this hand, Kearse was able to execute a pseudo-squeeze to bring home her slam. We know you would never fall for it, but would you be there to help your partner avoid the trap as well?

West dealer
Both sides vulnerable

North
♠ K 9 8
♡ A 10 5
◇ **A**
♣ A K Q J 8 5

East (you)
♠ Q 4
♡ K J 4
◇ Q J 10 4 2
♣ 10 7 2

◇ 3

| 6NT |

West	North	East	South
pass	2 ◇*	pass	2 NT
pass	3 ♣	3 ◇	3 NT
pass	6 NT	(all pass)	

*game force

West leads the ◇ 3.

Kearse wins the ace in dummy and you play . . .

Now declarer leads a low heart from dummy. How do you defend?

Solution 8

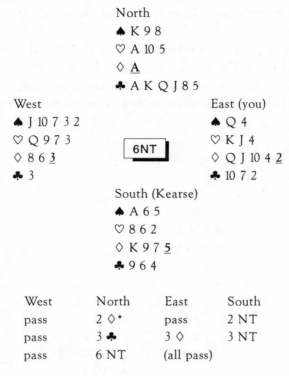

North
♠ K 9 8
♡ A 10 5
◇ **A**
♣ A K Q J 8 5

West
♠ J 10 7 3 2
♡ Q 9 7 3
◇ 8 6 <u>3</u>
♣ 3

6NT

East (you)
♠ Q 4
♡ K J 4
◇ Q J 10 4 <u>2</u>
♣ 10 7 2

South (Kearse)
♠ A 6 5
♡ 8 6 2
◇ K 9 7 <u>5</u>
♣ 9 6 4

West	North	East	South
pass	2 ◇*	pass	2 NT
pass	3 ♣	3 ◇	3 NT
pass	6 NT	(all pass)	

*game force

At the table, East followed low to the first trick, then rose with her ♡K at trick two. She then played back the ◇Q. Kearse won and ran her clubs. West pitched two spades, one heart and one diamond, but on the sixth round of clubs, she pitched a fatal spade, guarding her ♡Q-9.

East knows, if she's counting, that if declarer holds the ♡Q, declarer has 12 tricks (two spades, two hearts, two diamonds and six clubs). Therefore, East places West with the ♡Q. East also knows that only West can possibly guard spades. If only West can guard spades, East must guard hearts, and East must give violent suit preference for hearts.

One way to do this is to lead back the ◇J (based on the "jack is always suit preference for the lower suit" rule).

Another easy way is to follows in clubs with the 2, 7 and 10 —

a baby suit-preference signal for hearts.

If you went up with the ♡K and returned the ♡4 to clear West of her ♡Q, you made an even better play than signaling — as long as West is also counting declarer's tricks. However, if West fails to count and thinks you have the doubleton ♡K, she will play low on the heart, and the ♡10 will win!

It's too bad the game was matchpoints and not imps. With no fear of an overtrick, East could play the ♡4 on the lead of a heart from dummy. West wins and knows for sure where the ♡K is. If South has it, she has 12 tricks, so East *must* have it.

Problem 9

Do you have your trick-one signals down pat now? Try this one from the Bal Harbour Olympiad.

East dealer
Both sides vulnerable

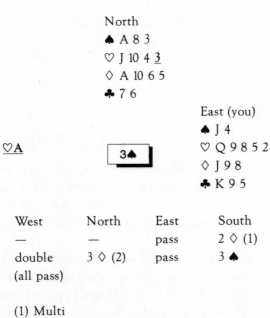

North
♠ A 8 3
♡ J 10 4 <u>3</u>
◇ A 10 6 5
♣ 7 6

East (you)
♠ J 4
♡ Q 9 8 5 2
◇ J 9 8
♣ K 9 5

♡A   3♠

West	North	East	South
—	—	pass	2 ◇ (1)
double	3 ◇ (2)	pass	3 ♠
(all pass)			

(1) Multi
(2) Bid your suit

West leads the ♡A (ace from ace-king) and you play . . .

Solution 9

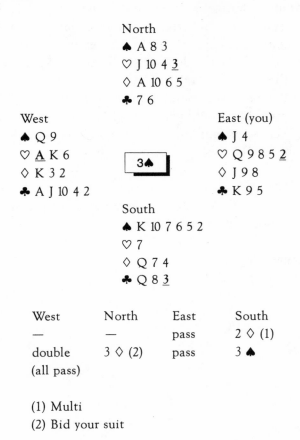

North
♠ A 8 3
♡ J 10 4 <u>3</u>
♢ A 10 6 5
♣ 7 6

West
♠ Q 9
♡ <u>A</u> K 6
♢ K 3 2
♣ A J 10 4 2

East (you)
♠ J 4
♡ Q 9 8 5 <u>2</u>
♢ J 9 8
♣ K 9 5

3♠

South
♠ K 10 7 6 5 2
♡ 7
♢ Q 7 4
♣ Q 8 <u>3</u>

West	North	East	South
—	—	pass	2 ◇ (1)
double	3 ◇ (2)	pass	3 ♠
(all pass)			

(1) Multi
(2) Bid your suit

It looks like declarer should lose one heart, two diamonds and two clubs, but the internationalists sitting East-West failed to defeat the contract. West led a high heart and switched to . . . the ◇2. Devastating. Now declarer had six spades, two diamonds and a club ruff for +140.

Using obvious-shift methods, East follows to the first heart with the ♡2. West switches to a low club and the defense plays three rounds of clubs. Declarer ruffs the third club and pulls trumps, but cannot avoid the two diamond losers.

Problem 10

New Orleans Pairs Olympiad 1978
North dealer
East-West vulnerable

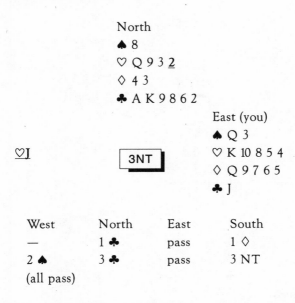

North
♠ 8
♡ Q 9 3 <u>2</u>
♢ 4 3
♣ A K 9 8 6 2

East (you)
♠ Q 3
♡ K 10 8 5 4
♢ Q 9 7 6 5
♣ J

♡J

3NT

West	North	East	South
—	1 ♣	pass	1 ♢
2 ♠	3 ♣	pass	3 NT
(all pass)			

North's opening bid was light, to say the least. And you might have raised partner's spades. Now you must rely on accurate defense.

West leads the ♡J, the 2 from dummy, and you . . .

Solution 10

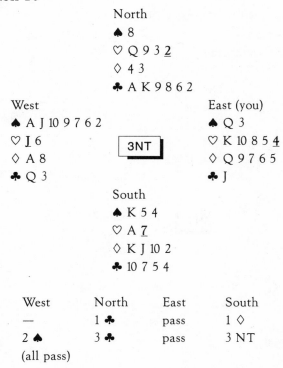

North
♠ 8
♡ Q 9 3 2
♢ 4 3
♣ A K 9 8 6 2

West
♠ A J 10 9 7 6 2
♡ J 6
♢ A 8
♣ Q 3

3NT

East (you)
♠ Q 3
♡ K 10 8 5 4
♢ Q 9 7 6 5
♣ J

South
♠ K 5 4
♡ A 7
♢ K J 10 2
♣ 10 7 5 4

West	North	East	South
—	1 ♣	pass	1 ♢
2 ♠	3 ♣	pass	3 NT
(all pass)			

West led the ♡J, trying not to give away the ninth trick in spades. Had he led a spade, declarer would have had only eight tricks, however. East gave an encouraging signal in hearts, South ducked, and West continued with another heart. Declarer played a club to the ace, and a diamond to the 10, and suddenly the contract was cold.

East has a tough play at trick one, because though he has help for his partner in spades, the Obvious Shift, he certainly wants a second heart played if declarer wins the ♡A and later puts West back on play. But he has time to signal the ♡K. He *doesn't* have time to signal a spade card, if declarer ducks the first trick. East must play the ♡4 at trick one. When South ducks, West can now switch to a spade, for down one.

If declarer wins the first heart and leads a club to dummy for a diamond play, East will follow with the ♢5, to indicate that he holds the ♡K as well as the spade honor he advertised at trick one.

Problem 11

New Orleans Venice Cup
West dealer
Neither side vulnerable

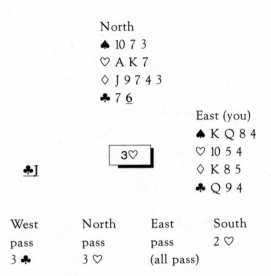

North
♠ 10 7 3
♡ A K 7
◇ J 9 7 4 3
♣ 7 6

East (you)
♠ K Q 8 4
♡ 10 5 4
◇ K 8 5
♣ Q 9 4

3♡

♣J

West	North	East	South
pass	pass	pass	2 ♡
3 ♣	3 ♡	(all pass)	

West leads the ♣J. You play . . . and declarer wins the ace. She leads the ♡9 to partner's 6 and dummy's king, while you follow with . . .

Solution 11

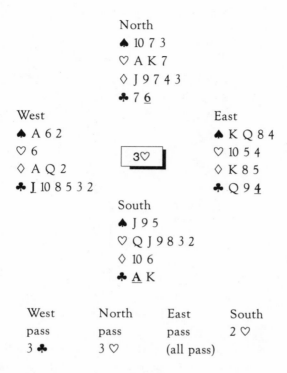

North
- ♠ 10 7 3
- ♡ A K 7
- ◇ J 9 7 4 3
- ♣ 7 <u>6</u>

West
- ♠ A 6 2
- ♡ 6
- ◇ A Q 2
- ♣ <u>J</u> 10 8 5 3 2

East
- ♠ K Q 8 4
- ♡ 10 5 4
- ◇ K 8 5
- ♣ Q 9 <u>4</u>

3♡

South
- ♠ J 9 5
- ♡ Q J 9 8 3 2
- ◇ 10 6
- ♣ <u>A</u> K

West	North	East	South
pass	pass	pass	2 ♡
3 ♣	3 ♡	(all pass)	

In the final of the New Orleans Venice Cup, the American North-South was allowed to score +170 on a hand where the defense had five top tricks.

West led the ♣J. Declarer won the ace, played the ♡9 to the king, and a small diamond to the 5, 6 and queen. East-West were using upside-down count signals, and West played her partner to hold a doubleton diamond. Therefore, she continued with the ace and another diamond. Declarer ruffed and was able to pitch two spades on dummy's diamonds.

When East and South followed to the second round of diamonds, West should know her partner does not hold a doubleton. If she began with only two small diamonds, declarer would have started with ◇K-10-6 and would hardly play a diamond to the 6 at trick three!

Let's look at what cards East should play at trick one and two. First, East should follow with the ♣4, saying she doesn't like clubs but likes the Obvious Switch (spades). Second, she should follow to the first trump with the ♡5, beginning a suit preference for spades. (The ♡10 signal is a bit dangerous, because it presents declarer with a third trump entry to dummy.)

Question: Should West switch to spades after winning the ◊ Q?

Answer: No. The spade tricks can't go away, so why not continue clubs and simply wait to see if East wins the second round of diamonds? Then East can switch to spades, which will be much better if she holds something like ♠K-J-9-x. Common sense here says return a club with the West hand, no matter what East signals.

Problem 12

Here is deal from the team event in New Orleans. Which card would you play at trick one against a five-club contract?

South dealer
East-West vulnerable

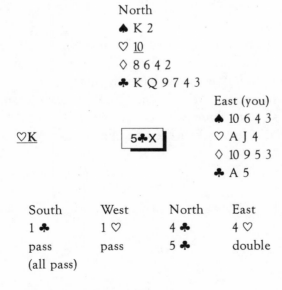

North
♠ K 2
♡ 10
◊ 8 6 4 2
♣ K Q 9 7 4 3

East (you)
♠ 10 6 4 3
♡ A J 4
◊ 10 9 5 3
♣ A 5

♡K

5♣X

South	West	North	East
1 ♣	1 ♡	4 ♣	4 ♡
pass	pass	5 ♣	double
(all pass)			

West leads the ♡K. What is your play?

Solution 12

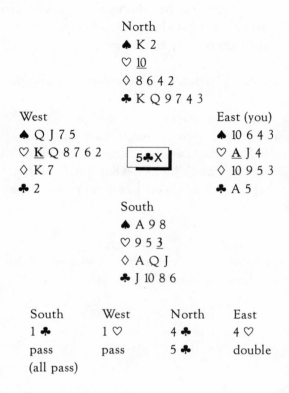

North
♠ K 2
♡ <u>10</u>
◇ 8 6 4 2
♣ K Q 9 7 4 3

West
♠ Q J 7 5
♡ <u>K</u> Q 8 7 6 2
◇ K 7
♣ 2

5♣X

East (you)
♠ 10 6 4 3
♡ <u>A</u> J 4
◇ 10 9 5 3
♣ A 5

South
♠ A 9 8
♡ 9 5 <u>3</u>
◇ A Q J
♣ J 10 8 6

South	West	North	East
1 ♣	1 ♡	4 ♣	4 ♡
pass	pass	5 ♣	double
(all pass)			

This one should be easy; overtake the heart and switch to a diamond. At the table, East played the ♡4. Was it count, suit preference or attitude? West must have thought it was attitude, because he switched to the ◇K, reasoning that his partner must be able to stand a shift to dummy's weaker suit or he would have either encouraged or overtaken the opening lead.

Problem 13

New Orleans Rosenblum Teams
North dealer
Both sides vulnerable

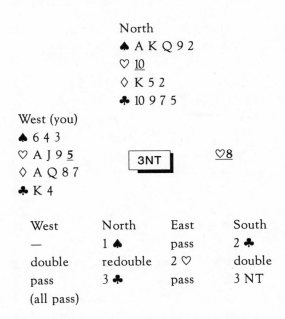

                    North
                    ♠ A K Q 9 2
                    ♡ 10
                    ◇ K 5 2
                    ♣ 10 9 7 5

West (you)
♠ 6 4 3
♡ A J 9 5   ┌─────┐   ♡ 8
◇ A Q 8 7   │ 3NT │
♣ K 4   └─────┘

West	North	East	South
—	1 ♠	pass	2 ♣
double	redouble	2 ♡	double
pass	3 ♣	pass	3 NT
(all pass)			

You lead the ♡5. Dummy's 10 wins, partner playing the 8 and declarer the deuce. Declarer plays four rounds of spades, discarding one heart, one diamond and one club, while partner follows ♠5, 7, J, 10, winning the fourth spade. You discard a diamond on the fourth spade and partner returns the ♡4, queen from South, ace. You lead the ♡J, East following with the 6, and declarer wins the king. Two clubs have been discarded from dummy on the hearts. Declarer now leads the ◇3.

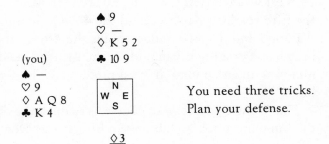

                    ♠ 9
                    ♡ —
                    ◇ K 5 2
(you)   ♣ 10 9
♠ —
♡ 9
◇ A Q 8   ┌───────┐   You need three tricks.
♣ K 4   │   N   │   Plan your defense.
             │ W   E │
             │   S   │
             └───────┘

                    ◇ 3

Solution 13

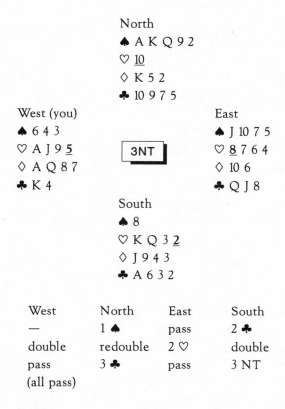

North
♠ A K Q 9 2
♡ 10
◇ K 5 2
♣ 10 9 7 5

West (you)
♠ 6 4 3
♡ A J 9 5
◇ A Q 8 7
♣ K 4

3NT

East
♠ J 10 7 5
♡ 8 7 6 4
◇ 10 6
♣ Q J 8

South
♠ 8
♡ K Q 3 2
◇ J 9 4 3
♣ A 6 3 2

West	North	East	South
—	1 ♠	pass	2 ♣
double	redouble	2 ♡	double
pass	3 ♣	pass	3 NT
(all pass)			

The Brazilian East-West pair was unable to defeat Poland's vulnerable three notrump. Poland went on to win the Rosenblum Cup.

At the crucial stage, when declarer led a diamond up, West, a world champion, won the ace and returned the queen, and that was that.

West was worried that if he ducked, he would be squeezed on the fifth spade, if declarer held the ♣A-Q. Suppose he ducks the diamond and declarer indeed holds the ♣A-Q; if West pitches a high heart or a high diamond on the fifth spade, declarer throws him in with a diamond. If West pitches a club, declarer drops his king.

The winning defense, of course, is to duck the diamond toward the king and pitch a club on the fifth spade. Declarer takes four spades, two hearts, one diamond and one club. West cannot afford to rise with the ◊ A and shift to a club because East's ◊ 10 can then be pinned by South's jack.

The duck of the diamond lead is easy when you know partner, not declarer, holds the ♣Q. Partner should play a high heart at trick one. He has no honors in the suit, but you already know that because he couldn't cover dummy's ♡10. Thus, the high heart shows no tolerance for the Obvious Shift (diamonds). Next East follows to the spades beginning with his lowest, the 5, 7, J and 10, indicating a preference for clubs but not a fabulous holding, or he would have continued straight up the line. His return of the ♡4 can also help remind West that clubs is where his strength lies.

Problem 14

You are East in the Stockholm Bermuda Bowl.

South dealer
Neither side vulnerable

```
                        North
                        ♠ J 9 5 4
                        ♡ 10 8 4
                        ◊ A K J 5
                        ♣ K 2
                                        East (you)
                                        ♠ 10 8
              ┌──────┐                  ♡ —
              │  6♠  │                  ◊ Q 8 7 6 3 2
   ♣A         └──────┘                  ♣ 10 9 8 6 3
```

South	West	North	East
1 ♠	3 ♡	4 ♠	pass
4 NT	pass	5 ◊	pass
6 ♠	(all pass)		

Perhaps you should have made a Lightner double. But maybe that would have pushed them to a cold six notrump. In any case, you didn't double and now partner leads the ♣A. Your play . . .

Solution 14

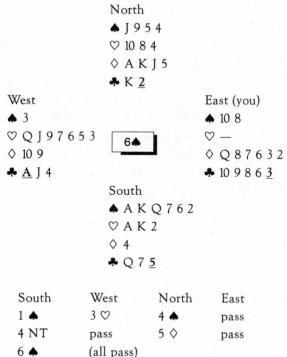

North
- ♠ J 9 5 4
- ♡ 10 8 4
- ◊ A K J 5
- ♣ K 2

West
- ♠ 3
- ♡ Q J 9 7 6 5 3
- ◊ 10 9
- ♣ A J 4

6♠

East (you)
- ♠ 10 8
- ♡ —
- ◊ Q 8 7 6 3 2
- ♣ 10 9 8 6 3

South
- ♠ A K Q 7 6 2
- ♡ A K 2
- ◊ 4
- ♣ Q 7 5

South	West	North	East
1 ♠	3 ♡	4 ♠	pass
4 NT	pass	5 ◊	pass
6 ♠	(all pass)		

Play the ♣3, asking for the Obvious Shift. In standard carding, players give suit preference for dummy's remaining two non-trump suits when no more tricks are possible in the suit led; here it would be the ♣10, suit preference for hearts. However, we use the Obvious-Shift carding *all the time* to keep signals consistent.

Warning: Don't revert to your old ways just because it *seems like* you can make a clearer signal. Under pressure, against a slam, players who adopt a method of carding will often relapse into their prior method. This is very dangerous ground. You must stick to your system no matter what.

Playing Obvious Shift, you simply (and always) make your two-step approach at trick one: (1) Identify the obvious shift; (2) Signal low for the switch, high for a continuation, and an honor for the *non-obvious shift*.

Problem 15

From "More Killing Defense at Bridge" by Hugh Kelsey*
North dealer
Neither side vulnerable

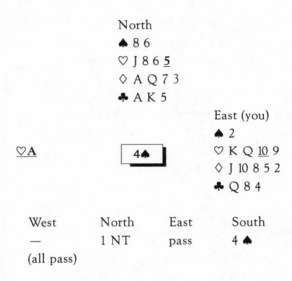

North
♠ 8 6
♡ J 8 6 <u>5</u>
◊ A Q 7 3
♣ A K 5

East (you)
♠ 2
♡ K Q <u>10</u> 9
◊ J 10 8 5 2
♣ Q 8 4

♡A   4♠

West	North	East	South
—	1 NT	pass	4 ♠
(all pass)			

"West begins with the ace and another heart, your ♡9 winning the second trick when dummy plays low. Declarer ruffs the third round of hearts and cashes the ♠A-K, partner following with the 5 and 7 while you discard the ◊2. The ♠J is then led to West's queen, the ♣5 discarded from dummy. What do you discard on this trick?"

That was Kelsey's problem. Playing obvious-shift/suit-preference methods, you get this problem:

West begins with the ♡A and ♡7, your 9 winning the second trick when dummy plays low. Declarer ruffs your ♡Q and cashes the ♠A-K, partner following with the 7 and 5, while you discard the ◊2. The ♠J is then led to West's queen, the ♣5 discarded from dummy. What do you discard on this trick?

*Faber & Faber, 1972.

Solution 15

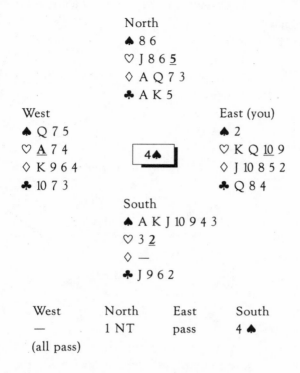

North
♠ 8 6
♡ J 8 6 <u>5</u>
◇ A Q 7 3
♣ A K 5

West
♠ Q 7 5
♡ <u>A</u> 7 4
◇ K 9 6 4
♣ 10 7 3

East (you)
♠ 2
♡ K Q <u>10</u> 9
◇ J 10 8 5 2
♣ Q 8 4

4♠

South
♠ A K J 10 9 4 3
♡ 3 <u>2</u>
◇ —
♣ J 9 6 2

West	North	East	South
—	1 NT	pass	4 ♠
(all pass)			

Kelsey's answer is that if declarer has seven spades, he can always finesse the ◇Q for his contract, so it won't help to keep your fourth diamond. If declarer has only six spades, partner will switch to a club after winning his spade trick and South will be unable to score 10 tricks unless he has the ◇K.

Playing suit preference, you don't have to think so deeply. Obviously you cannot let go of your fourth heart, and after partner warned you to guard clubs by following with the 7-5 of trumps, you cannot let go of a club.

Problem 16

Chagas-Branco were allowed to make 10 tricks in notrump on this deal. See if you can stop them.

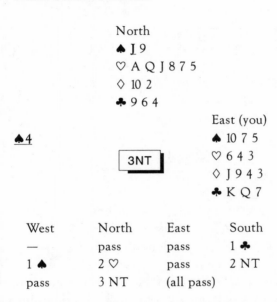

Geneva, Pair Olympiad
North dealer
North-South vulnerable

North
♠ J 9
♡ A Q J 8 7 5
◇ 10 2
♣ 9 6 4

♠ 4

3NT

East (you)
♠ 10 7 5
♡ 6 4 3
◇ J 9 4 3
♣ K Q 7

West	North	East	South
—	pass	pass	1 ♣
1 ♠	2 ♡	pass	2 NT
pass	3 NT	(all pass)	

West leads the ♠4 (fourth best) to dummy's jack and South's 3, while you follow with . . .

Declarer plays a club from dummy. You split with the king, losing to South's ace, partner following with the 8. Declarer leads a second club to dummy's 9 and your queen, partner playing the 5. Your play is . . .

Solution 16

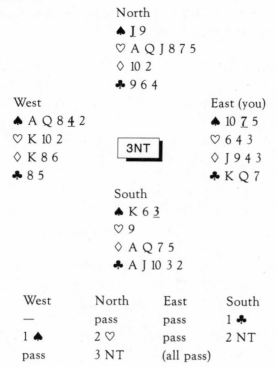

North
- ♠ J 9
- ♡ A Q J 8 7 5
- ◊ 10 2
- ♣ 9 6 4

West
- ♠ A Q 8 <u>4</u> 2
- ♡ K 10 2
- ◊ K 8 6
- ♣ 8 5

3NT

East (you)
- ♠ 10 <u>7</u> 5
- ♡ 6 4 3
- ◊ J 9 4 3
- ♣ K Q 7

South
- ♠ K 6 <u>3</u>
- ♡ 9
- ◊ A Q 7 5
- ♣ A J 10 3 2

West	North	East	South
—	pass	pass	1 ♣
1 ♠	2 ♡	pass	2 NT
pass	3 NT	(all pass)	

In real life, East switched to the ◊J to the queen and king. West returned a diamond. Declarer won dummy's 10 and ran his minor-suit winners. West was forced to come down to three hearts and the stiff ♠A. Declarer played a heart to the queen, then got out with a spade. West won and had to play a second heart to dummy's remaining ♡A-J, and the Brazilians scored +630.

When West follows to the two rounds of clubs with the 8-5, asking for a spade return, East cannot go wrong. The diamond shift would work only when West held the ◊A-Q-x-x. Though this is possible, it is not likely. Still, why waste energy on what *might* be when you have an easy signaling system to tell you what *is*? West's suit-preference play in clubs is all the information East needs.

Many pairs in this situation play Smith echo, in which a high-low by either defender in declarer's long suit shows interest in the suit led. This would also work here, but because our main method is suit preference, we do not need Smith echo.

Problem 17

This hand is from the round-robin match between the USA and Sweden in the Stockholm Bermuda Bowl.

North dealer
North-South vulnerable

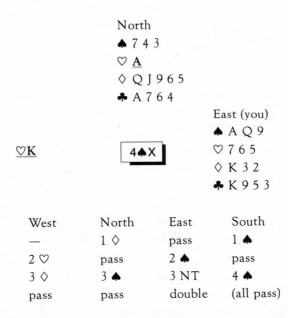

North
♠ 7 4 3
♡ **A**
◇ Q J 9 6 5
♣ A 7 6 4

East (you)
♠ A Q 9
♡ 7 6 5
◇ K 3 2
♣ K 9 5 3

♡K   4♠X

West	North	East	South
—	1 ◇	pass	1 ♠
2 ♡	pass	2 ♠	pass
3 ◇	3 ♠	3 NT	4 ♠
pass	pass	double	(all pass)

Your partner leads the ♡K, won in dummy. You play . . . as South follows with the 9. Declarer calls for a low diamond and you . . .

Solution 17

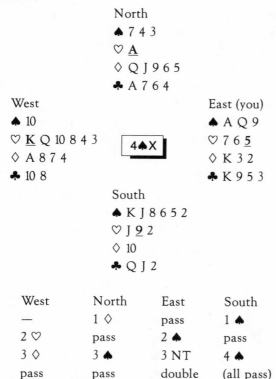

North
♠ 7 4 3
♡ **A**
♢ Q J 9 6 5
♣ A 7 6 4

West
♠ 10
♡ **K** Q 10 8 4 3
♢ A 8 7 4
♣ 10 8

4♠X

East (you)
♠ A Q 9
♡ 7 6 **5**
♢ K 3 2
♣ K 9 5 3

South
♠ K J 8 6 5 2
♡ J **9** 2
♢ 10
♣ Q J 2

West	North	East	South
—	1 ♢	pass	1 ♠
2 ♡	pass	2 ♠	pass
3 ♢	3 ♠	3 NT	4 ♠
pass	pass	double	(all pass)

West led the ♡K, won in dummy. Declarer called for a low diamond. East rose with his king (an excellent play) to lead the ♠A and a spade. (A heart return would have made life easier for the defense.)

Declarer won the jack, ruffed a heart with dummy's last trump, and played the ♢Q, discarding a heart from hand. West won and played . . . the ♡Q *instead of a club*, so the American declarer was able to ruff, pull the last trump and enter dummy with the ♣A to cash two good diamonds. He was ⁺790.

West played declarer to hold ♠ K J 8 6 5 2 ♡ J 9 7 2 ♢ 10 ♣ K 2. This would require some fancy falsecarding by declarer in the heart suit, and for East to have cuebid with:
♠ A Q 9 ♡ 6 5 ♢ K 3 2 ♣ Q J 9 5 3. Both are conceivable.

The important question is: Where could East have helped West in his carding?

East's ♡5 at trick one said he could stand a club shift. East clearly holds either the ♣K or ♣Q-J to have enough points for his bidding. His play to the second round of diamonds should clarify his club holding: The ◊2 shows the ♣K. There's nothing like a deuce for suit-preferencing — it's such a clear signal.

Problem 18

This was a beautiful defense by the Pakistani Team against the French in the Bal Harbour Rosenblum Cup. See if you can match it.

East dealer
North-South vulnerable

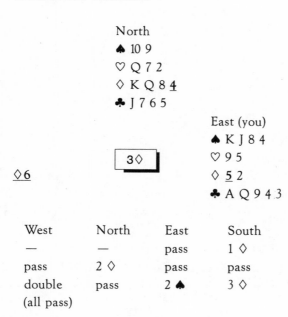

North
♠ 10 9
♡ Q 7 2
◊ K Q 8 4
♣ J 7 6 5

East (you)
♠ K J 8 4
♡ 9 5
◊ 5 2
♣ A Q 9 4 3

3◊

◊6

West	North	East	South
—	—	pass	1 ◊
pass	2 ◊	pass	pass
double	pass	2 ♠	3 ◊
(all pass)			

West leads the ◊6. Declarer wins in hand with the 9 and plays a low heart. West wins his king and plays a second trump, the ◊7. Declarer wins in dummy and plays the ♠10. You cover with the jack, and declarer plays the 3 as West follows with the 2. What do you play now?

Solution 18

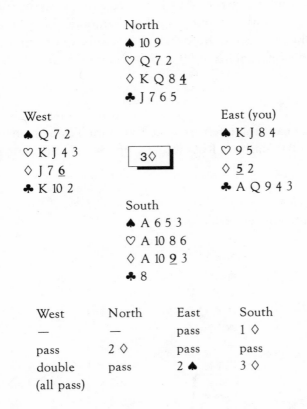

North
♠ 10 9
♡ Q 7 2
◇ K Q 8 4
♣ J 7 6 5

West
♠ Q 7 2
♡ K J 4 3
◇ J 7 6
♣ K 10 2

3◇

East (you)
♠ K J 8 4
♡ 9 5
◇ 5 2
♣ A Q 9 4 3

South
♠ A 6 5 3
♡ A 10 8 6
◇ A 10 9 3
♣ 8

West	North	East	South
—	—	pass	1 ◇
pass	2 ◇	pass	pass
double	pass	2 ♠	3 ◇
(all pass)			

In real life, East played a low club to West's king, allowing the defense to play a third round of trumps; this left declarer a trick short.

What were the two clues for East to underlead in clubs?

(1) When West led his second round of trumps, he led the 7, not a higher one.

(2) On the first round of spades West followed with the ♠2 — a clear signal that he holds the ♣K.

By the way, East begins with the ◇5 on the first trump play because with three suits to give suit preference for, he keys in on his bid suit (spades), while eliminating dummy's longest suit (clubs).

Problem 19

Stockholm Bermuda Bowl
South dealer
Neither side vulnerable

North
- ♠ J 10 8 6
- ♡ 7 2
- ◇ A J 6 4
- ♣ J 10 2

West (you)
- ♠ 9 5 4 2
- ♡ K Q 10 5 4
- ◇ Q 9
- ♣ 8 4

1NTX

♣7

South	West	North	East
1 ♡	pass	1 ♠	pass
1 NT	pass	pass	double
(all pass)			

As West, you lead the ♣8, on the sound theory, "against one notrump, lead passively, because you have plenty of time to set up your long suit, and you don't want to burn a trick on the first lead."

When you follow this principle, however, you must back it up with good carding, to help partner *find* your long suit! Once in a rubber bridge game in New York, two famous players, Phil Feldesman and Tobias Stone, doubled one notrump and the opening leader tried a passive lead, holding a side suit of six hearts to the ace-queen-jack! His partner gained the lead three times, and led back the three other suits; the contract made and the smoke from the postmortem lingers to this day.

Back to our hand. Let's suppose you find this ♣8 lead, dummy's ♣J holds as partner plays the 7 and South the 6. Declarer plays a spade to East's ♠3 and South's king, while you follow with . . .

Now a diamond is led. How do you defend?

Solution 19

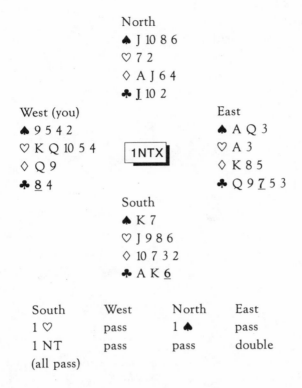

North
♠ J 10 8 6
♡ 7 2
◇ A J 6 4
♣ J 10 2

West (you)
♠ 9 5 4 2
♡ K Q 10 5 4
◇ Q 9
♣ 8 4

1NTX

East
♠ A Q 3
♡ A 3
◇ K 8 5
♣ Q 9 7 5 3

South
♠ K 7
♡ J 9 8 6
◇ 10 7 3 2
♣ A K 6

South	West	North	East
1 ♡	pass	1 ♠	pass
1 NT	pass	pass	double
(all pass)			

The Pakistani East-West were unable to defeat the Swedes in one-notrump doubled. After the ♣8 lead, dummy's ♣J held. Declarer played a spade to the king, and a diamond to the jack and king. East returned a club and declarer finished with one spade, three diamonds and three clubs, for +180.

West must begin "screaming" for a heart shift as soon as possible. How can he tell East where his suit is?

He can do this simply by following suit to spades and diamonds with his highest cards. Declarer plays a spade to his king, and West follows with the ♠9. Declarer leads a diamond toward dummy and West follows with the ◇Q. Even if West fails to put up the ◇Q, the heart shift should be obvious to East after the ♠9 play. East-West will finish with two spades, five hearts and one diamond, for +300.

Problem 20

You are in the Semifinals of the Bermuda Bowl.
It is the last board.
You don't know it, but your team is leading by 9 imps.
If you can defeat this contract, you reach the final.
Can you do it?

VuGraph Room
East dealer
East-West vulnerable

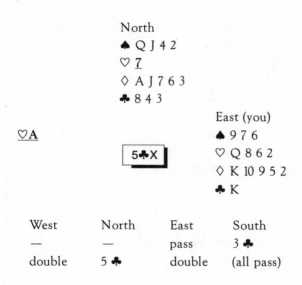

North
♠ Q J 4 2
♡ 7
◇ A J 7 6 3
♣ 8 4 3

♡A

5♣X

East (you)
♠ 9 7 6
♡ Q 8 6 2
◇ K 10 9 5 2
♣ K

West	North	East	South
—	—	pass	3 ♣
double	5 ♣	double	(all pass)

West leads the ♡A.
What do you play on the first trick?

Welcome back to where we began this book on page 4. If you recall, the deal occurred at the world championships in Santiago, Chile, 1993. Norway was 9 imps behind Brazil with one deal to go.

East dealer
East-West vulnerable

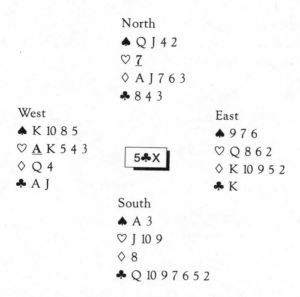

North
♠ Q J 4 2
♡ 7
◇ A J 7 6 3
♣ 8 4 3

West
♠ K 10 8 5
♡ A K 5 4 3
◇ Q 4
♣ A J

5♣X

East
♠ 9 7 6
♡ Q 8 6 2
◇ K 10 9 5 2
♣ K

South
♠ A 3
♡ J 10 9
◇ 8
♣ Q 10 9 7 6 5 2

Closed Room Result: 5♣ doubled by South, down 1, +100 for Norway

Open Room

West	North	East	South
—	—	pass	3 ♣
double	5 ♣	double	(all pass)

When the Open-Room auction flashed on the VuGraph screen, most of the kibitzers in the audience assumed the match was decided. All Brazil had to do was defeat the contract one trick, and, as you can see, the defense had at least two trump tricks, at least one heart trick and was due to score a spade trick as well.

Then the following scenario took place. The West player for Brazil led the ♡A. The East player signaled with the deuce. What could go wrong now? Suddenly West got the idea to play ace and another trump. He led the ♣A — aghh! The trump honors crashed. But it was not over. If West continued trumps or switched to diamonds or hearts, he would still score his ♠K for the setting trick.

West began to think. Could declarer have the ◇K? What did that ♡2 mean at trick one? Who had the ♠A?

After a pause, the final blow for the defense came. West shifted to the ♠8 and the Norwegian declarer scored 11 tricks to win the match by 3 imps.

Okay, readers. It is now one year and 179 pages later. For Obvious-Shift pros, this deal is a cinch, right?

Question: What is the Obvious Shift?

Answer: Spades, dummy's shorter side suit.

Question: What should East play at trick one?

Answer: The ♡8, encouraging, asking partner not to make the spade switch. The ♡Q is also a possible signal, demanding a diamond shift, but risky and not necessary when a simple, encouraging signal will do.

Note that West, who wasn't sure which suit to shift to, had control of trumps. So he could have saved the day by applying the "two-chances-are-better-than-one" defense. After winning the first trick, he could switch first to diamonds and see what his partner signals. Then, if partner does not like diamonds, West can switch to spades when in with the ♣A.

Did you make it to the world championship final by helping partner with the ♡8 signal? Someday . . .

Thank you for reading

A Switch in Time

We hope you've enjoyed it!

 To order another copy, see page 186.

Rules for Identifying the Obvious Shift
in order of priority

Negatives

(A) The Obvious Shift cannot be the suit led.

(B) The Obvious Shift is never trumps.

(C) The Obvious Shift is never a suit headed by the A-K-Q or four of the top five honors.

(D) The Obvious Shift in a suit contract is never dummy's singleton or void.

(E) The Obvious Shift is never a natural suit bid by declarer.

Positives

(1) The opening leader's bid suit is the Obvious Shift.

(2) If the opening leader has not bid a suit, the leader's partner's bid suit is the Obvious Shift.

(3) If both defenders have bid suits and the opening leader starts with an unbid suit, look at the suits and choose one of them by applying the rules below.

When the defense has bid two suits or when the defense has not bid any suits . . .

(4) Against a suit contract, a three-card suit headed by at most one honor (A, K, Q, J, 10) is the Obvious Shift. Against notrump, dummy's shortest suit is the Obvious Shift (even a strong holding such as ace-king doubleton).

(5) When there is no weak three-card suit, the shortest suit is the Obvious Shift. But against a suit contract, this cannot be a singleton or void.

(6) When there are two equal-length suits, either of which might be the Obvious Shift, look at the number of honors. The suit with fewer honors is the Obvious Shift. If the suits have an equal number of honors, the lower-ranking suit is arbitrarily deemed to be the Obvious Shift.

A Switch in Time

$12.95 each plus $3 shipping and handling per order (US funds)

To order another copy for your partner . . .

with a credit card:
phone 216-371-5849   or   fax 216-371-2941

with a check or money order, write to:
Granovetter Books
3194 Oak Rd
Cleveland Hts OH 44118

Rules for Identifying the Obvious Shift
in order of priority

Negatives

(A) The Obvious Shift cannot be the suit led.

(B) The Obvious Shift is never trumps.

(C) The Obvious Shift is never a suit headed by the A-K-Q or four of the top five honors.

(D) The Obvious Shift in a suit contract is never dummy's singleton or void.

(E) The Obvious Shift is never a natural suit bid by declarer.

Positives

(1) The opening leader's bid suit is the Obvious Shift.

(2) If the opening leader has not bid a suit, the leader's partner's bid suit is the Obvious Shift.

(3) If both defenders have bid suits and the opening leader starts with an unbid suit, look at the suits and choose one of them by applying the rules below.

When the defense has bid two suits or when the defense has not bid any suits . . .

(4) Against a suit contract, a three-card suit headed by at most one honor (A, K, Q, J, 10) is the Obvious Shift. Against notrump, dummy's shortest suit is the Obvious Shift (even a strong holding such as ace-king doubleton).

(5) When there is no weak three-card suit, the shortest suit is the Obvious Shift. But against a suit contract, this cannot be a singleton or void.

(6) When there are two equal-length suits, either of which might be the Obvious Shift, look at the number of honors. The suit with fewer honors is the Obvious Shift. If the suits have an equal number of honors, the lower-ranking suit is arbitrarily deemed to be the Obvious Shift.

A Switch in Time

$12.95 each plus $3 shipping and handling per order (US funds)

To order this book . . .

with a credit card:
phone 216-371-5849   or   fax 216-371-2941

with a check or money order, write to:
Granovetter Books
3194 Oak Rd
Cleveland Hts OH 44118

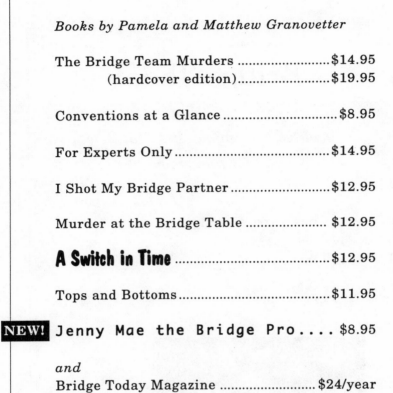

Notes

Notes